Sandy
LaMastus

J. L. Ladd Fagerson
(purchased July 28, 1987
in Billings Montana
at the Greyhound Bus
Depot for 25¢)

You & your thoughts

The power of right thinking

EARL D. RADMACHER

Tyndale House
Publishers, Inc.
Wheaton, Illinois
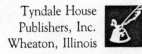

Library of Congress Catalog Card Number 77-77358. ISBN
0-8423-8570-3, paper. Copyright © 1977 by Tyndale House
Publishers, Inc., Wheaton, Illinois. All rights reserved. First printing,
June 1977. Printed in the United States of America.

CONTENTS

It's time to reopen abandoned minds

"Thar's gold in them thar hills!"

I can't give you the name and social security number of the grizzly old prospector who first made that famous, though ungrammatical, declaration over a century ago. I can tell you, however, that his startling announcement plunged the American West into a most colorful and exciting era. His words reached beyond the West, into the small towns of the Plains, and as far east as Boston and Philadelphia. Almost overnight, farmers, businessmen, drifters and cowpokes poured into the "strike zone" in search of the precious metal that would bring them fame and fortune.

A lot of history has gone by the board since the Gold Rush days. Many boom towns are only ghost towns today, and not far from them are old mines—abandoned and deteriorating. Their wooden doors and beams may creak in the wind, but mostly the mines bear silent, somewhat eerie testimony to bygone glory. Old-timers insist there's still gold to be scooped out of some of the abandoned mines, but the cost of getting the gold out would exceed its value.

It seems to me that the human mind has met a fate similar to that of deserted mines. We have left the Age of Reason far behind and are living in what I choose to call the Age of Unreason. Philosophers in the Age of Reason regarded the human mind as a valid authority for testing all things. In the Age of Unreason, feelings command the highest honors, according to many of our contemporaries. Both ideas are wrong, but if we Christians are going to relate God's Word effectively to modern society, we must understand this phenomenon.

A couple of years ago, Melvin Maddocks, a contributing writer to *Time* magazine, captured the mood of our day. In his essay "The New Cult of Madness: Thinking As a Bad Habit," Maddocks observed: "'Reason' and 'logic' have, in fact, become dirty words—death words. They have been replaced by the life words 'feeling' and 'impulse.' Consciousness—the rational—is presumed to be shallow and unconsciousness—the irrational—to be always interesting, often profound, and usually *true.*"

I recall another article, "Just the Feelings, Man" by Wayne C. Booth, a rhetoric professor at the University of Chicago. "We are in a time of intellectual crisis," Booth observed, "a time when confidence in reason is so low that most men no longer try to provide good reasons for what they believe."

Booth told of an English professor's explanation of his standards for accepting articles for *Modern Philology*. "I can't really insist on anything that could be called a 'standard,'" the professor explained. "I'm happy if I can find essays which show *some* kind of connection between the conclusions and the evidence offered."

In the same article Booth commented that "if you read closely in McLuhan, Brown, and many other contemporaries, you will find that they are expressing a dissatisfaction with reason that goes far beyond a simple mistrust of logic or 'linear thinking.' At its extreme it is a repudiation of thinking at all, in favor of feeling or of the 'wisdom of the body.'"

Feelings, then, seem to be in the driver's seat, as it becomes increasingly common to lay the brain aside and let feelings and impulses make decisions for us. And this certainly shows in our shopping habits. In his book *The Hidden Persuaders,* Vance Packard points out that well over 90 percent of the purchases made in the United States are based on emotion and impulse.

What are these men—Maddocks, the rhetoric prof, and Packard—trying to tell us? Simply this: modern man has hung an "Out to Lunch" sign over his brains. The implication is clear: our society is heading for serious trouble unless it stops to think. No civilization can function satisfactorily in a mindless vacuum. But, as I see it, the greatest problem concerns us Christians. If we take on the thought patterns of the society in which we live, the result will be absolutely disastrous. We'll have lost our ability to decide what is true and right on the basis of objective revelation—the Bible. Instead, we'll be floundering around in a sea of emotions, not knowing where to drop anchor.

If this danger seems remote, let me remind you that a recent best seller in the Christian community was *Like a Mighty Wind* by Mel Tari, a well-known convert of the Indonesian revival. A provocative question was raised in Mel Tari's book: "Can the Indonesian revival be reduplicated in America?" The answer was given: "Yes, if you will take out that small computer which is your brain, put it in a little box, and shoot it to the moon, and then let God use your heart." A popular saying that expresses the same idea is, "A man who has an experience is never at the mercy of a man who has an argument."

If we took that philosophy seriously, we would have to rewrite the Bible. For example, whereas Isaiah 1:18 declares, "Come now, and let us reason together," we would have to insist upon "Come now, and let us feel together." Or consider Peter's instructions in his first epistle: "Sanctify the Lord God in your hearts: and be ready always to give an answer to every man that asketh you a reason of the hope that is in you" (3:15). We would have to adjust Peter's words to read, "… be ready always to dump your emotions on every man that asketh you a reason of the hope that is in you." And we would object vehemently to Paul's announcement in 2 Timothy 1:7 that God has given us "a sound mind." We would much prefer to say that God has given us "good vibes."

Of course, not everyone agrees with Mel Tari's apparent disdain for an intelligent approach to the Christian life. For example, in his book *Your Mind Matters* John Stott, internationally renowned Christian clergyman, issues a clear warning about the advancing tide of anti-intellectualism. He submits: "Anti-intellectualism in the church is again occurring with growing frequency. The present generation of young people are activists, and experience has become important over against truth. Experience without truth is the menace and misery of mindless Christianity."

Francis A. Schaeffer, too, voices concern over the growing tendency to elevate feelings—experience—to the throne of authority. In his volume *The New Superspirituality* Schaeffer cautions: "Beware! Neither experience nor emotion is the basis of faith. The basis for our faith is that certain things are true. The whole man, including the intellect, is to act upon the fact that certain things are true. That, of course, will lead to an experiential relationship with God, but the basis is content not experience."

Schaeffer continues: "We must stress that the basis for our faith is neither experience nor emotion but truth as God has given it in verbalized, propositional form in the Scriptures, and which we first of all apprehend with our mind, though, of course, the whole man must act upon."

Let me share with you a most poignant excerpt

from *The Authority of the Bible* by Don Miller. I consider it an outstanding note of caution regarding putting our confidence in experience. "Experience in itself is too subjective, too inner, too changeable, too fleeting, too tied to physiological factors to be a trustworthy guide for faith. To trust our experience is to put our faith at the mercy of our liver, or our endocrine glands, or the quality of our sleep on any given night, or the state of our digestion, or the state of mind of other members of the family, or the problems of our work. Experience must always be subjected to the authority of the saving work of God in Jesus Christ set forth in the Bible." Miller concludes: "What we need, then, is not the authority of experience, but the experience of authority."

What these men are saying is valid, for there is no certainty of truth in the profundity of experience. Our actions must be based on the absolute truth.

And isn't this precisely what Jesus Christ endeavored to get across to those who wanted to be his disciples? Do you recall his dramatic words in John 8:32? "Ye shall know the truth, and the truth shall make you free." Make no mistake about it—truth leads to the experience of being free; any experience not based on truth results not in freedom but enslavement!

You've heard the old maxim that "birds of a feather flock together." Well, occasionally birds of different feathers flock together. I'm referring to the phenomenon of certain religious leaders and the irreligious psychologist B. F. Skinner sharing the concept that behavior is based on something other than intellectual response to propositional truth.

Skinner, as leader of "behavioristic" psychology, considers man to be like a machine, bereft of what we Christians would call the "inner man." Pictured on the cover of *Time* (September 20, 1971), Skinner theorizes that actions are determined by the environment; behavior "is shaped and maintained by its consequences." The "inner man," according to Skinner, is a superstition that started with a false belief in man's inability to understand his world. With the rise of behavioral science, understanding has grown, and man no longer needs such fictions as "something going on inside the individual, states of mind, feelings, purposes, expectancies and all that."

Those who buy what Skinner and other behavioral psychologists are selling boast: "Tell us what kind of man you want: rich man, poor man, beggar man, thief, and we'll develop that man by manipulating the environmental factors which influence him."

You can see from all of this that a vigorous attack against Christianity is under way in our society. You can understand why Melvin Maddocks concluded in *Time* that reason and logic have become dirty words. The big question is, how shall we meet this attack? By throwing logic and reason out the window and going along with the popular mood? Or shall we refuse to be driven to who knows where by our feelings and impulses and, instead, exercise our God-given ability to think and choose our destiny and our daily steps? Let's pick the latter option and get behind the movement to *reopen abandoned minds*.

What 2 you think is what you are

GIGO. Sounds like a Greek verb, doesn't it? Or is it an Italian food you haven't tried yet? Well, before you reach for a Greek lexicon or rush to the nearest Italian restaurant, let me assure you it is neither of these. GIGO is a computer term, an acronym for *Garbage In, Garbage Out.* Computer programmers know that whatever they feed into a computer will inevitably show up in the printout. So, if "garbage" goes in, "garbage" will come out—GIGO.

The human mind is a fabulous computer. As a matter of fact, no one has been able to design a computer as intricate and efficient as the human mind. Consider this: your brain is capable of recording 800 memories per second for seventy-five years without ever getting tired. Although there are a number of computers on the market today with amazing capabilities packed into them, not one of them can match the service record of the human brain. God has certainly placed a phenomenal, one-of-a-kind piece of equipment in the human cranium.

Now, here's something on the plus side for the average computer: its engineers and programmers, understanding the meaning of GIGO, do their dead-level best to keep "garbage" out of the program so they do not get "garbage" in the printout. Human beings, on the other hand, don't exercise very much care about what they feed into God's computer, the brain. It's amazing how much "garbage" some persons will program into their brains as they sit for hours in front of the TV. It has been estimated that by the time a person in our society reaches the age of eighteen he has watched 25,000 hours of television, including 350,000 commercials. (You know how intellectually stimulating commercials are!)

Am I overly concerned about the adverse effect of television on the human mind? I don't think so. Some time ago I was reading *Media and Methods,* the stock and trade magazine for communications people, when I came across a provocative statement by Herbert Marshall McLuhan, who is a giant in the field of communications. McLuhan affirmed, "Only madmen would use television if they knew the consequences."

Certainly the Bible confirms the principle that what we feed into our minds will come out in the life. We can place McLuhan's alarming observation about TV squarely in line with what King Solomon observed about 3,000 years ago. "As he thinketh in his heart, so is he," Solomon wrote in Proverbs 23:7.

In that twenty-third chapter of Proverbs we find wise King Solomon giving some cogent advice to a man who is about to be conned into a bad deal. He portrays a situation in which a rich, prestigious ruler wants to swindle a dinner guest. In order to accomplish the rip-off, the rich man pretends to be sincerely interested in his guest. As soon as he gets what he wants, though, he'll drop him like a hot potato. King Solomon counsels, "Don't go by appearances. Things are not always what they seem to be. A man isn't necessarily what he says or does. His speech and actions may be contrived to fool you. In the final analysis, only what lies deep inside the counsels of a man's heart presents a true picture of what the man is."

You know how this works, don't you? A person can put on a big smile and shake hands with another person, pretending to care, when he really doesn't have two cents worth of interest in the other person. Maybe you have been the other person a time or two, and consequently you have learned not to go just by what you see on the surface. You get the point Solomon makes: "as he thinketh in his heart, so is he."

Let me explain that word *heart,* because it had a different meaning when the Bible was written than it has today. You might tell someone, "I love you with all my heart," but in Bible times you would have said, "I love you with all my kidneys," or, "I love you with all my bowels." You see, in Bible times the kidneys and bowels were regarded as the center of human affection, whereas the heart was regarded as the center of reflection. What Solomon was driving at, then, when he advised, "As he thinketh in his heart, so is he," is simply this: "As a man thinks in the center of his deepest reflection, that's what he will be." The things he thinks about deeply are the raw materials which form his actions.

With this in mind, consider what another king—King David—volunteered in verse 11 of Psalm 119, which is the richest chapter in the Word of God *about* the Word of God. "Thy word have I hid in mine heart, that I might not sin against thee," David testified.

Perhaps you memorized this verse a long time ago. I learned it when I was a kid. It was part of a memorization project I was working on to win a free week at camp. The project involved memorizing about eighty or ninety verses. So I started with "Jesus wept," then moved on to "Rejoice evermore," then tackled "Pray without ceasing." That gave me three. Camp still seemed to be a long way off! Finally, I got around to Psalm 119:11: "Thy word have I hid in mine heart, that I might not sin against thee." I plugged that verse into my memory, but I never gave the slightest thought to what it was really saying. Now I consider it one of the most profound bits of biblical psychology you and I will ever encounter.

Think about Psalm 119:11: "Thy word [concepts, words, input] have I hid [that is, have

I tucked away in the innermost recesses of my being], that I might not sin against thee." David's inspired words tell me that what I plug into the reflective center of my being will be the raw material out of which my actions come. Good reason to feed Scripture rather than "garbage" into your divinely built-in computer, don't you agree?

I have heard some persons complain that their brain is too tired to get involved in a program of Scripture memorization. I have news for them—the body can get tired, but the brain never does. A human being doesn't use more than 2 percent of his brain power, scientists tell us. And, of course, some demonstrate this fact more obviously than others. The point is, the brain is capable of an incredible amount of work and it retains everything it takes in. You never really forget anything; you just don't recall it. Everything is on permanent file in your brain.

Fortunately, I don't recall everything I've fed into my head. I used to complain about not having a good memory until I began to remember some of the stuff I'd forgotten. When I was in the seventh grade I had the distinct, but dubious, honor in the school of being able to swear the longest without using the same swear word twice. I really thank God that I can't recall those words now. The Word of God, you see, has had a cleansing effect upon my innermost thought life since I became a Christian.

Do you recall Jesus' words in John 15:3? They

draw our attention to the cleansing job the Scriptures perform in our lives. Jesus announced, "Now ye are clean through the word which I have spoken unto you." The word for "clean" in this verse comes from the Greek word *katharismos* from which we get our English word "catharsis." Jesus Christ employs the Word to give us a mental catharsis; and, if you will pardon the frank language, it's similar to what we do to our bowels when we get an enema. The Scriptures act as an enema for the brain. David certainly appreciated the cathartic effect of Scripture, for he counseled: "Wherewithal shall a young man cleanse his way? By taking heed thereto according to thy word" (Psalm 119:9).

The subject of washing comes up in a most interesting head-on collision involving the scribes and Pharisees and Jesus Christ. The opening verses of Matthew 15 carry the story: "Then came to Jesus scribes and Pharisees, which were of Jerusalem, saying, Why do thy disciples transgress the tradition of the elders? for they wash not their hands when they eat bread."

Were these religious figures really concerned about sanitary eating habits? Not at all. Their real hang-up was the complex list of picky rules governing Jewish life, which appeared in the *Babylonian Talmud*. There were even rules about how the Jews were supposed to wash their hands. The scribes and Pharisees called "Foul!" because Jesus' disciples weren't observing the rules.

Just how complicated were those man-made

rules? Rabbi Solomon Ganzfried discusses the "Code of Jewish Law" governing hand-washing in his book *A Compilation of Jewish Laws and Customs:*

> The ritual hand-washing in the morning is performed as follows: Take a cup of water with the right hand and put it in the left; pour some water upon the right hand. Take the cup back in the right hand and pour some water on the left. This performance is repeated three times. It is best to pour the water over the hands as far as the wrists, but in case of emergency it suffices if the water covers the hands up to the joints of the fingers. One must also wash his face in honor of the Creator, as it is said (Genesis 9:6): "For in the image of God he hath made the man." One must also rinse the mouth, because we must pronounce the Great Name in purity and cleanliness. Afterward the hands are dried. Special care must be taken to dry the face thoroughly.
>
> The hands must be washed into a vessel only. The water thus used must not be utilized for any other purpose, because an evil spirit rests on it (contaminated, and injurious to health), and it must not be spilt in a place frequented by human beings.
>
> Before the morning hand-washing, one should not touch either the mouth, the nose, the eyes, the ears, the lower orifice, or any kind of food, or an open vein,

because the evil spirit that rests upon the hands before washing them will cause injury to these things.

It is best to perform the morning ablution with water poured from a vessel by human effort, just as it must be done when washing the hands before meals.... But in case of emergency, and one wishes to pray, one may wash his hands in any manner, even when the water is not poured by human effort, and one may pronounce the benediction: *Al netilat yadayim* (concerning the washing of the hands). If there is a river or snow at hand, one should dip the hand in it three times. If, however, there is no water in any form available, one may wipe one's hands with some material, and say the benediction: "Blessed art ... for *cleansing* (not *washing*) the hands." Afterwards, upon finding water and the required vessel, one must wash the hands properly without pronouncing any benediction.

The Pharisees, then, wanted to know why Jesus' disciples didn't follow the hand-washing rules. Jesus' answer was really a question: "Why do ye also transgress the commandment of God by your tradition?" (verse 3). "Ye hypocrites," he continued, "well did Esaias (Isaiah) prophesy of you, saying, This people draweth nigh unto me with their mouth, and honoureth me with their lips, but their heart is far from me. But in vain they do worship me, teaching for doctrines the commandments of men" (verses 7-9).

Then Jesus summoned the multitude and instructed: "Hear, and understand" (verse 10). Understand what? Namely, an extremely significant principle. "Not that which goeth into the mouth defileth a man; but that which cometh out of the mouth, this defileth a man" (verse 11).

The Pharisees didn't appreciate this principle one bit, for it focused on what a man is inside as the important thing. They just weren't about to start any kind of exploratory surgery to discover what they were really like internally. They were only concerned with external forms and ceremonies. The Scripture informs us that they were offended by Jesus' words (verse 12).

It was Peter who brought the news to Jesus that the Pharisees were offended. Good old Peter! What did he expect the Pharisees to do—give Jesus the Man-of-the-Year Award? But in spite of Peter's apparent concern that his Master had offended the Pharisees, I thank God for Peter. You see, he asked the Lord to explain the principle he had just stated. (If I'd been there I would have wondered about the meaning, too.)

So the Lord gave Peter a crash course in Anatomy 101. In verse 17 his explanation went like this: "Peter, don't you understand how the body works? Whatever enters the mouth goes into the stomach, is digested, and eventually is eliminated from the body. It ends up in the dung heap." Then he gave the spiritual application in verses 18 and 19: "The things which proceed out of the mouth come from the heart—the inner man—and they defile him. These impure things include evil thoughts, murders, adultery, fornication, theft, lying, and blasphemy."

Do you get the picture? The Pharisees took great precautions to cleanse their hands before eating. They were meticulous about external observances, but they were filthy inside. Why? Because they refused to let the Word of God penetrate into their innermost being and do its cleansing work.

You might ask, How do the kinds of impurities Jesus mentioned get into the heart? Here's how—through the ear gate and through the eye gate. The evil we program into our minds permeates our innermost being, spreading impurity and corruption. Then these things which defile us come gushing out and flood our speech and conduct, thereby defiling others.

A few years ago Stuart Chase's article "How Language Shapes Our Thoughts" appeared in *Harper's*, emphasizing how closely language and thoughts are integrated. According to Chase, language "molds one's whole outlook on life," for "thinking follows the tracks laid down in one's language." Knowing about this integration of language and thoughts helps us to understand that what we say often reflects what we are. The state of our heart and mind will show up in our words, for "out of the abundance of the heart the mouth speaketh" (Matthew 12:34).

The Apostle James deals with this truth in verses

13-15 of the first chapter of his epistle. He holds back nothing in telling us that what we really are inside will show up in our overt acts. After a brief discussion about enduring temptation, he insists: "Let no man say when he is tempted, I am tempted of God: for God cannot be tempted with evil, neither tempteth he any man."

D. G. Kehl provides an excellent observation about temptation in "Sneaky Stimuli and How to Resist Them" (*Christianity Today*, January 31, 1975). He writes:

> Many Christians have a simplistic concept of temptation that goes something like this: Satan, at a particular moment, flits to our side and whispers "Do it," and we either do or do not, depending upon our spiritual strength at that moment. We might be more consistently victorious in *not* "doing it" if we realized that there is much more to temptation than the overt, momentary solicitation to evil and that our strength or weakness at that moment is based upon attitudes that have been forming for weeks, months, even years prior.
>
> We do not fall in a moment; the predisposition to yield to sin has been forming, building, germinating—but not necessarily consciously so. Sin has both a cumulative and a domino effect. Satan plants subtle stimuli, often subliminal ones; he influences an attitude; he wins a "minor"

victory—always in preparation for the "big" fall, the iron-bound habit. The words of James support such a view: "Every man is tempted, when he is drawn away of his own lust, and enticed. Then *when lust hath conceived, it bringeth forth sin ...*" (James 1:14, 15). It is the time between "conceiving" and "bringing forth," that shadowy interim between stimulus and response, that may be largely subliminal.

What does this have to do with overt sinning? Simply this—James 1:13-15 makes it abundantly clear that a Christian has no right to pin the blame on God when he sins. He can't accuse, "Look here, God; I was doing just fine until you put me into an impossible situation. It's all your fault!"

Based on James' explanation of the "evolution" of sin from temptation to the bitter consequences of sinning, I draw the following conclusion: when, as a child of God, I walk in sin, I am giving evidence that I have short-circuited fellowship between God and me. (The meaning of "death" in James 1:15 must be separation—broken fellowship—not physical death, because people sin regularly without physical death resulting.) Some Christians get confused at this point. They suppose that God severs fellowship when a believer sins. Actually, a believer sins because he had already broken fellowship with God. He wouldn't have sinned if he had stayed in fellowship with God.

James' words make it clear to me that my fellowship with God depends upon what I allow to enter my ear gate and eye gate. I simply can't afford to be indiscriminate. If I program "garbage" in, "garbage" will come out. I must attach a high priority to getting into the Word of God, which will clean my mind and give me a proper understanding of what God is like.

That's a meaningful priority. Matthew 4:4 is vitally important: "Man shall not live by bread alone, but by every word that proceedeth out of the mouth of God." Do we Christians have time to eat daily, but no time to get into the Word? Do we have time to read the newspaper every day, but not the Bible? Time enough to glue ourselves to the TV set, but no time for the Scriptures? What does all of this say about our values?

If your values are fouled up, may I suggest you give some thought to the New Testament word *repentance.* It's made up of two little words in the Greek language: *meta* and *noeo.* Together, they mean "after to think," or "to have a change of mind, to have a second thought." But, interestingly, whenever "repentance" occurs in the New Testament, it includes a change of action. You see, there isn't really a change of mind unless there is a corresponding change of action. If you have filled your mind with undesirable thoughts, change your mind and change your action. Stop neglecting the Word; start programming it into your mind. It will make a difference.

Well-known psychologist Gordon Allport would

agree that a person's thought life exerts a profound influence on his conduct. He believes, "An attitude is a mental and neural state of readiness, organized through experience, exerting a directive or dynamic influence upon the individual's response to all objects and situations with which it is related." An attitude, therefore, is a state of mind toward a value. Consequently, it seems to me that any genuinely dynamic Christian life will be the outgrowth of a dynamic Christian attitude, shaped and locked into our thinking by the Word of God. And any faulty, unproductive Christian life will be the outgrowth of attitudes shaped and locked into our thinking by an unholy world system. This is the age-old relationship of cause and effect, root and fruit, a belief that behaves and an attitude which acts.

Taking all of this into consideration, I discover that I must program Scripture into my heart. The end product of this is the fruit of the Spirit (Galatians 5:22, 23). But if I do not build Scripture into my mind and heart, the satanic world system's influences have uncontrolled access to my mind and heart. I then will be captivated by every sensation. I become a victim of my environment. Instead of the fruit of the Spirit, the product of the flesh results, which is thorns and thistles.

As I see it, some Christians resemble a pressure cooker with the lid ready to blow off. They have permitted the satanic world system to pump more and more pressure into their thought lives: selfish

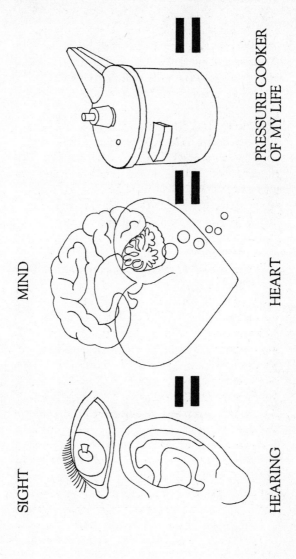

SIGHT

MIND

HEARING

HEART

PRESSURE COOKER
OF MY LIFE

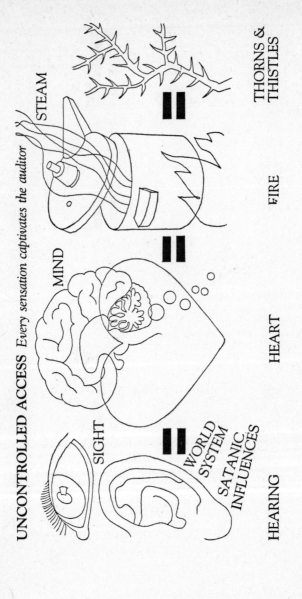

UNCONTROLLED ACCESS *Every sensation captivates the auditor*

HEARING · SIGHT = WORLD SYSTEM SATANIC INFLUENCES

MIND = HEART

STEAM = FIRE

THORNS & THISTLES

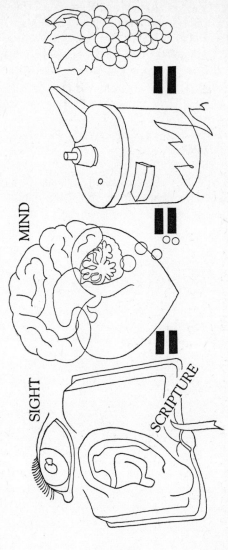

CONTROLLED ACCESS *Auditor captivates every sensation*

SIGHT

MIND

FRUIT

SCRIPTURE

HEARING

ambitions, worry, lust, anger, resentment, fear.
They suppose that adding heavier lids will keep
these things from exploding into their behavior.
They are mistaken, of course, because eventually
the heaviest lid will blow and the blast will be
enormous.

Obviously, the answer doesn't lie with external
restraints. If we think it does, we are no wiser
than the Pharisees. The only way to withstand
the influences of a satanic world is to fill our
thoughts with God's Word. This will counteract the
pressures we face, keep us cool, and hold the lid on.

Take a look at your life. What you think is
what you are.

Where 3
right
thinking
begins

Unless you have been marooned on a remote Pacific island for the past five years and this book just happened to reach you via a bottle that washed ashore, you know there's an energy crisis under way. We are being urged to conserve energy. Natural resources are running low while fuel prices and frustrations are running high. There is at least one natural resource, though, which doesn't seem to be overdrawn. It is *mental energy.*

In the first two chapters, I insisted that many voices in our society—even in our churches—are clamoring for a revolt against a reasoning faith, a faith based upon propositional truth—the Bible. Their revolt is aimed at elevating emotional experience to the throne of authority over our lives. And I registered my objection to this mood, calling instead for a revival of thinking—serious thinking—in which God's Word gets programmed into the innermost center of our being. My reason for wanting this to happen is clear: our actions are the product of our thinking.

I hope you are concerned enough about the quality of your life to want to think right. You may ask, How can I think right? I would suggest to you that the starting point for right thinking is to think right about what God is like. You see, "The fear of the Lord is the beginning of knowledge" (Proverbs 1:7). Also, "The fear of the Lord is the beginning of wisdom" (Proverbs 9:10). Both knowledge (familiarity with facts) and wisdom (correct application of facts) derive from right thinking about God.

Right thinking about God is the logical place to begin, is it not? If God is the Creator who made man in his image, then a study of God is the proper basis for learning about man and his world. I realize, of course, that humanists would object, insisting that we must study man himself if we are going to understand man and his world. But humanists will never open the door to a true understanding of the nature of man without the only key to that door. The key is knowing what God like. So the proper study of man is not *man*; the proper study of man is *God*.

Isaiah, chapter 6, portrays this truth beautifully. The prophet Isaiah shares with us how he entered the Temple one day and saw the Lord—high, holy, and lifted up. The Lord's train filled the Temple, and the angels surrounding his throne ascribed praise to him. "Holy, holy, holy, is the Lord of hosts: the whole earth is full of his glory," they exclaimed. That remarkable disclosure of God's glorious and holy character made an immediate impact on Isaiah's thinking. Understanding in a new way what God is like, Isaiah got a true picture of himself. "Woe is me!" he lamented, "for I am undone; because I am a man of unclean lips, and I dwell in the midst of a people of unclean lips."

But Isaiah also saw grace and mercy in God. God dispatched an angel to carry a live coal from the altar, lay it on the prophet's mouth, and purge his lips. Isaiah was prepared then to offer himself to God for service. He volunteered, "Here am I; send me." A correct view of God had provided the foundation upon which Isaiah could build a meaningful life.

The first and most important factor in right thinking and right living, then, is to get a correct view of God—to understand what he is like. But where will I look to see him?

You may suggest, "I'll set my sights for God in nature. Up in the mountains, among the tall pines, where the air is fresh and zesty—that's where I'll get a fantastic picture of God!" I would submit that you could learn something about God from that vantage point, but your picture of him would be inadequate. You see, while you were drinking in the beauty of the high country, nature's face might be getting some ugly scars elsewhere. An earthquake might be splitting the ground open in Guatemala. A tornado might be uprooting trees and crops in a Midwestern county. A tidal wave might be engulfing villages in the Philippines.

And I must remind you that such catastrophes are called "acts of God." If you observed these "acts of God," your picture of God would likely be quite different.

The point is, nature cannot give us an adequate concept of God, because the world you and I look at is distorted and twisted. God did not make it that way. He created a perfect environment for man, but man ruined that environment by rebelling against God. World history and upheavals in nature tell the sad story of the results of man's sin in the midst of God's creation. So when we look at nature and history alone to provide a picture of God, we get a distorted view.

Not long ago I was reading the thin volume *Lessons of History* in which the famous historian Will Durant portrays some of the most severe natural disasters our world has witnessed. Based on his investigation of those disasters, he concludes that history is no more prejudiced in favor of Jesus Christ than of Genghis Khan. I believe Durant's conclusion is wrong because he views history from a faulty perspective. The right way to look at history is through the perspective of an interpretation of history called the Bible. Without the Bible I would surely study the raw data of history, look at natural disasters—like an earthquake in Guatemala—and wonder, How could a loving God do such things to innocent people? With the Bible, I see what God is like. I learn that he is absolutely trustworthy. Although I cannot understand everything that goes on in the world, I derive assurance from the Bible that God's ways are perfectly holy and wholly perfect.

Do you know what we need today? More books expounding the biblical doctrine of God. Even though about a thousand books a day are being published, the books on this subject could be counted on the fingers of one hand. We need books like *The Knowledge of the Holy* by A. W. Tozer, who preached and wrote of God's character a generation ago. Tozer's book is full of solid spiritual food. You can feed your soul as you read his pages on God's immutability, holiness, and sovereignty.

More recently, *Knowing God* by J. I. Packer of Bristol, England, has come off the presses to stretch our understanding of the person of God. It even has a handbook which goes with it to help readers get through it, because so many Christians can't absorb such solid reading material without help. I've been through Packer's book three times and consider it one of the most helpful books I've ever read. It has contributed a great deal to my life.

Another book which deals with the nature of God in a substantial manner is *The Attributes of God*, by A. W. Pink. It is older than either Tozer's or Packer's book, but it is worth adding to your library and your life. But, having mentioned those three books, I have just about exhausted the contemporary contribution to this lofty subject. If I want to read beyond Tozer, Packer, and Pink in the category of what God is like, I must go all the way back to the writings of the Puritans in early

America. There I find many books about the character of God. Most of them have not survived the passing of time, but a few concerned entrepreneurs have underwritten the cost of reprinting some of them. One of these valuable reprints is the 900-page *The Existence and Attributes of God* by Stephen Charnock.

It isn't a very exciting title, is it?—*The Existence and Attributes of God*. Who could get excited about reading a book with such a dull title? Furthermore, its 900 pages have only two kinds of print—fine and finer! But let me guarantee you this—you will profit from every paragraph. You'll find yourself picking up that book in the morning; you will read two or three paragraphs and be so overwhelmed with its blessings that you will put it down again and spend the rest of the day thinking about those paragraphs.

I guess it's only fitting that we go through *The Existence and Attributes of God* slowly, pensively, and reverently. After all, Charnock wrote it slowly, pensively, and reverently. He made it his practice to get up very early every morning to write a couple of pages on what God is like. Is there any wonder there's something really substantial in what he communicates to us about God?

Several years ago I received a phone call from a pastor in the East. The first thing he said to me was, "I finished it!"

"I beg your pardon," I countered. "Who is this? What did you finish?"

He explained, "Remember two years ago you

spoke at a pastors' conference in New Jersey? You told about the book by Charnock, *The Existence and Attributes of God,* and said many Christians don't have the mental fortitude to read through a book like Charnock's. Well, you really got to me. I decided I would show you that I could take on Charnock's book. After the conference I got that book. I've been reading in it every day for the past two years. I finished the last page today, and I wanted you to be the first to know. It has been one of the richest spiritual feasts I have known outside of Scripture."

What does all of that indicate? It says that Puritan America had some spiritual giants who knew what God was like. They filled their thinking with lofty concepts and the results showed in the Great Awakening, which was probably the greatest revival America has ever experienced. In that era a man like Jonathan Edwards—college president, preacher, teacher, minister to Indians out in the wilderness, writer of in-depth theology—could stand in his pulpit, appear tall and lean, round-shouldered, beady-eyed, and without a lot of theatrics read a theological manuscript to a congregation and pack a spiritual wallop. One of his famous addresses has been preserved for us. It is "Sinners in the Hands of an Angry God." Historians tell us people clung to the pews as Jonathan Edwards preached that famous sermon. They were reluctant to let go of the pews for fear of slipping and dropping into Hell before the sermon ended. They waited in agony for

Jonathan Edwards to reach a point in the sermon where they could catch sight of the Savior and find deliverance in him.

Obviously Jonathan Edwards' mind and heart were filled with the knowledge of what God is like. He had caught the same truth that captured John Calvin previously. In his *Institutes of the Christian Religion* Calvin wrote: "... it is certain that man never achieves a clear knowledge of himself unless he has first looked upon God's face, and then descends from contemplating him to scrutinize himself." Edwards preached the sovereignty and holiness of God. Consequently, his congregation learned what God is like.

And the whole town learned about God, too. In one of Jonathan Edwards' works, *Faithful Narrative of the Surprizing Work of God,* written in 1737, he points out that there was "universal interest in religion. It affected the whole town. Scarcely a person has been exempt" from spiritual influence. He goes on to say that "our church, I believe, was the largest in New England before, but persons lately have thronged in, so that there are very few adult persons left out." At one point Edwards reports "great multitudes converted," and talks about eighty and 100 persons at a time coming into the membership of his church. In one six-month period there were over 300 converts. No wonder historians refer to the phenomenon of Jonathan Edwards' ministry as the Great Awakening!

I hear so many suggest that what we need

today is a revival, and I agree—we do need a revival. But I must admit—it is doubtful that we shall see a revival like the Great Awakening until we have the kind of preaching on the nature of God that characterized Puritan America. You won't find a foundation for revival in trivial preaching, spiritually anemic literature, or much of our contemporary music. We must get back to a serious pursuit of the person of God as revealed in Scripture.

Until we understand who God really is, our lives will not be all that different from what they have been. Right living begins with right thinking. And right thinking begins with thinking right about God.

A 4
perfect
picture
of God

Where can you find a perfect picture of God? You will be shortchanged if you try to find it in nature. And even the best writings of Puritan theologians—as helpful as they are—present only a partial picture of God. I submit to you that there is only one place where you can find a fully adequate, undistorted, perfect picture of God. It is in the person of Jesus Christ.

This is precisely what the Apostle John tries to get across to us in the first chapter of his Gospel. Perhaps you recall how he describes Jesus Christ in verses 1-13. He portrays him as the eternal Word—the *Logos*—who was in the beginning with God. He points out that the Word was God, the Creator of all things. Then, in verse 14, he drops a profound theological concept into our gray matter: "The Word was made flesh, and dwelt among us, (and we beheld his glory, the glory as of the only begotten of the Father), full of grace and truth." Jesus Christ, the eternal *Logos*, by means of the Incarnation visited our planet; he lived among men as perfect Man and perfect God. He pitched his tabernacle on earth, and John declares that he and others looked at the incarnated Word and saw divine glory and truth.

The record continues. Verses 15-18 offer, "John [the Baptizer] bore witness of him, and cried, saying, This was he of whom I spake, He that cometh after me is preferred before me: for he was before me. And of his fulness have all we received, and grace for grace. For the law was given by Moses, but grace and truth came by Jesus Christ. No man hath seen God at any time; the only begotten Son, which is in the bosom of the Father, he hath declared him."

Do you catch the significance of all this? When John writes that Jesus Christ is "in the bosom of the Father," he means that the Son of God is right next to the Father's heart. Therefore, he alone understands the Father well enough to portray him for us. We may safely say, then, that the only begotten Son of God is the exegesis, the exposition, and the explanation of what God is like. He is *the* God-manifestation. A perfect picture of God!

Hebrews, chapter 1, casts Jesus Christ in the same role. We read, "God, who at sundry times and in divers [various] manners spake in time past unto the fathers by the prophets, hath in these last days spoken unto us by his Son, whom he hath appointed heir of all things, by whom also he made the worlds; who being the brightness of his glory, and the express image of his person, and upholding all things by the word of his power, when he had by himself purged our sins, sat down on the right hand of the Majesty on high" (verses 1-3).

Two expressions in verse 3 are replete with meaning: "the brightness of his glory," and "the express image of his person." The first may be translated, *the effulgence of his glory,* suggesting that Christ is to the Father what rays of the sun are to the sun. The sun's rays share the exact qualities of the sun itself. Even so, Jesus Christ shares the same qualities of deity which the Father possesses. He is the effulgence of the Father, the overflowing of the Father.

The second expression, "the express image of his person," is analagous to a king's signet ring. When a king of that day pushed his signet ring into soft wax, he made his imprint there. That imprint was the "express image" of what appeared on the king's ring. Even so, Jesus Christ is the "imprint" of the Father.

You will find the same kind of focus on the Son of God in 2 Corinthians 3, where Paul volunteers that believers in the Church Age enjoy a privilege beyond what Israel under the law of Moses experienced. Under law, a heavy veil in the Temple separated the Jews from God. Christians, however, have direct access to God through Jesus Christ, who in his death and resurrection obliterated the veil. Paul insists that we Christians behold God's glory with an unveiled face. Here are his exact words: "But we all, with open [unveiled] face beholding as in a mirror the glory of the Lord, are changed into the same image from glory to glory, even as by the Spirit of the Lord" (verse 18). That "glory," as we have discovered from John's Gospel and Hebrews, is communicated in the person of Jesus Christ.

Let's put together what we have learned up to this point. 1) Jesus Christ is the incarnation of God. 2) He is the overflowing of the Father. 3) He is the express image of the Father. 4) He declares the glory of God. 5) We ought to look at Jesus Christ. This last point is stressed throughout the New Testament Epistles. Hebrews 12:2 urges us to be "looking unto Jesus." Verse 3 commands, "Consider him." Philippians 2 exhorts us to have the mind of Christ. First Peter 2:21 tells us to "follow his steps." And 1 John 2:6 advises, "He that saith he abideth in him ought himself also so to walk, even as he walked."

The Epistles, you see, drive us to the Gospels, for we view the life of Jesus Christ in the Gospels. I find this fascinating. It shows that the Gospels are the epitome of revelation, contrary to the opinion of many that revelation begins in the Old Testament, continues through the Gospels, and reaches its highest point in the Epistles. Actually, the Old Testament prophets led up to the Gospels and the apostles explained the Gospels in their epistles.

In the Gospels we see Jesus Christ as the only one who perfectly practiced what he preached. His righteous living complemented his teaching about righteousness. He not only brought the Word of God, he was the Word of God. A study of his life unlocks the mystery about what God is like.

Personally, I'm glad that we must depend on the four Gospels for our picture of Jesus Christ. Today people get into all kinds of arguments about Jesus' physical appearance. They debate whether he wore a crew cut or long hair, whether he had a clean-shaven face or wore a beard, whether his eyes were dark brown or light brown. It seems to me that God very wisely chose not to include an artist's sketch of his Son in the Bible, because he didn't want us to imprison the Lord of lords in a picture. Rather, he determined that we should derive our picture of his Son from his Son's words and actions.

Again, let me remind you that Paul tells us in 2 Corinthians 3:18 that we ought to behold Jesus Christ. The idea is, we should be steadfastly beholding him. The word "beholding" is in the present tense, which signifies a steady kind of action—looking at him, looking at him, looking at him.... The more you and I look at him, the more we become like him.

One extremely important fact: you must have spiritual life if you are going to look at Jesus Christ, if this kind of looking is going to be productive. Obviously, a dead person can't look at anything. So you must be a born-again person—a made-alive-in-Christ kind of person—before you can engage in the process of beholding Jesus Christ. Then you can focus your attention on him and look, and look, and look some more.

I must confess to you there was a time when looking at Christ was out of the question for me. Although I grew up in a church, it wasn't until I was fourteen that I trusted in Christ as my Savior. And it wasn't until I was twenty that I bothered to begin to study the Scriptures. Between the ages of fourteen and twenty I was living on experiences instead of God's authoritative Word.

What happened when I was twenty that made me decide to begin to study the Bible? I attended a Billy Graham Crusade in Portland, Oregon, and became convinced that God was calling me to preach. So I dedicated my life to Jesus Christ.

Does that sound kind of stupid? I guess from a secular viewpoint it does. I dedicated my life for now and for eternity to a person I'd never seen. But more than this, I have had the audacity to go and speak to thousands of other persons about Christ and encourage them to commit themselves to someone whom neither they nor I have ever seen. I have asked them to build a life of faith not sight.

Fortunately, I can derive support for my actions from an incident described in John 20. It involves Doubting Thomas. (I don't think we'll call him Doubting Thomas when we see him in Heaven, but he often gets that handle now.) He had not been with the disciples when Jesus appeared to them after his resurrection. So when the disciples claimed, "We have seen the Lord," Thomas insisted, "I'm from Missouri. I have to see it to believe it!" John records Thomas' exact words: "Except I shall see in his hands the print of the nails, and put my finger into the print of the nails, and thrust my hand into his side, I will not believe" (verse 25). Then, eight days later, Thomas got his chance. Jesus appeared to his disciples when Thomas was with them.

It was certainly a dramatic meeting. The doors were locked, yet somehow Jesus entered the room and "stood in the midst" (verse 26). It is interesting how the Lord slipped that miracle into the Gospel of John without elaborating on how he got into the room. Jesus said, "Peace be unto you," then followed his salutation with a directive to Thomas: "Reach hither thy finger, and behold my hands; and reach hither thy hand, and thrust it into my side: and be not faithless, but believing."

What was Thomas' response? He cried, "My Lord and my God." He saw, and he believed.

But the story doesn't end there. Jesus' subsequent statement is for you and me and everyone else whose life postdates Jesus' life on this planet. "Blessed are they that have not seen, and yet have believed." You see, Jesus Christ didn't break into human history just to satisfy the curiosity of one generation. Nor did he die and rise from the dead just for the benefit of one generation. He came to earth, lived, died, and rose from the dead for us all. And the Gospels record the whole story so that we who cannot see him may read about him and commit ourselves to him by faith.

But let's get back to Paul's emphasis in 2 Corinthians 3:18 to "beholding as in a glass [mirror] the glory of the Lord." What happens when we spend time—lots of time—looking at Jesus Christ by studying the Scriptures? Paul explains, "[We] are changed into the same image from glory to glory, even as by the Spirit of the Lord."

Do you see the principle involved in 2 Corinthians 3:18? We become like the object of our attention. Sad to say, the devil has some pretty sharp tricks in his asbestos bag. He has managed to get a lot of people, even some Christians, to spend more time studying demonology than Christology. Consequently, they know more about the devil than they do about Christ. Is it any wonder their lives are messed up?

May I suggest to you that you don't become more like the Savior by looking at Satan. The Treasury Department knows that you don't have to study the counterfeit in order to recognize the counterfeit. Treasury agents never see a phony bill during their training. But they do see and study the real thing, so much so that when they finish their training they can smell a counterfeit.

A woman in cancer research told me about this same sort of thing in her line of work. "We don't study cancerous tissue. We study healthy tissue. In this way we can detect cancerous tissues when they come along," she explained.

You can understand, then, why Paul tells us that looking and looking and looking at Christ changes us into the very image of Christ himself. And how appropriate that Paul used a word for "changed" which has given us our English word *metamorphosis*. As Christians, we are undergoing a metamorphosis as we become like Christ.

Sid was an ugly caterpillar with orange eyes. He spent his life groveling and squirming in the dirt on God's earth. One day Sid got a terrific idea. He crawled up the stem of a bush, made his way to a branch, and secreted a translucent fluid onto that branch. He made a kind of button out of the fluid, turned himself around, and attached his posterior anatomy to that button. Then he shaped himself into a "J," curled up, and proceeded to build a house around himself. There was a lot of activity for awhile, but before long Sid was entirely covered up and you couldn't see him anymore.

Everything became very, very still. You might have concluded that nothing at all was happening. But, as a matter of fact, plenty was happening. Metamorphosis was taking place.

One day Sid began to raise the window shades of his house. He let you look in and see a variety of colors. On another day an eruption took place. Sid's house shook violently. That little cocoon jerked and shook until a large, beautiful wing protruded from one of the windows. Sid stretched it out in all its glory. He continued his work until another gorgeous wing emerged from a window on the other side of the house.

At this stage of Sid's life you might have wanted to help. But you didn't, for if you tried to pull the rest of Sid's house off you would maim him for the rest of his life. So you let Sid convulse and wriggle his way to freedom without any outside intervention.

Eventually Sid got his house off his back, ventured out onto the branch, stretched, and spread his beautiful wings. He was nothing like the old worm he used to be. And do you know what? Sid didn't crawl back down the bush and start groveling and squirming in the dirt again. No indeed! Instead, he took off with a new kind of power—flight power. Now, instead of swallowing dust, Sid flies from flower to flower, enjoying the sweet nectar in God's wonderful creation.

The metamorphosis we experience as Christians is far better than Sid's. When you and I spend time with the raw materials of Scripture which form a portrait of Jesus Christ, the Holy Spirit uses those raw materials to fashion us into Christlikeness. It isn't an overnight project. It isn't accomplished in a week or two. (I realize that in a day of instant pudding, instant tea, instant coffee, and instant everything else, it isn't popular to insist that there is no such thing as instant spiritual maturity.) Paul indicates in 2 Corinthians 3:18 that the Spirit changes us from "glory to glory." He could have inserted 6,000 more glories if he'd had enough room to write them, but he gave us a sufficient number to show us that spiritual maturity isn't reached in one jump.

Someday our metamorphosis will be complete. We shall bear the image of the Lord without any human imperfections marring that image. Let's not lose sight of the goal, and let's remember—right thinking starts, continues, and concludes by thinking right about what God is like, as revealed in Jesus Christ.

The battle 5 for your mind

I suppose it would be a nice bit of good news if I told you the devil takes his hands off when you trust in Jesus Christ. But the fact is, he doesn't. As a matter of fact, he begins to work even harder than ever when you trust in Christ.

You say, "That doesn't make sense. Why should the devil waste his time on someone he's already lost for eternity?" Let me answer by reminding you that you aren't his chief target; Jesus Christ is. Although he has lost you for eternity, he hasn't lost you for time. Before you enter eternity he's going to pull out all the stops to get you off the track. He's going to work overtime to try to get you to dishonor your Lord. You see, he hates Jesus Christ because of what Jesus Christ did to him at the cross.

The church at Corinth provides an awesome example of how the devil works through believers to discredit the Savior. Unfortunately, the Apostle Paul, who wrote to the Corinthian church about their problems, never really got through to them. After he finished his first letter, he learned they were still suffering defeat at the hands of the evil one. So he corresponded with them in a second letter. As you read that second letter, you can't fail to see how hardhearted the Corinthian Christians were. In response to Paul's first letter they had disciplined a wicked brother, but in spite of the brother's subsequent repentance the Corinthians weren't willing to forgive and forget.

Isn't it incredible how they had gone from the extreme of not caring at first about how much sinning was going on in the church to the extreme of shunning the one who repented? Small wonder Paul gets near the end of his second letter and says something like, "You Corinthians are lucky you're not standing right here. If you were, I'd bust you one right in the nose!" (That's not precisely how Paul would have dispensed apostolic discipline, but you get the idea.) Cf. 2 Corinthians 13:2, 10.

Why were the Christians at Corinth so carnal? Because there was a battle going on for their minds and the devil was winning the battle. For one thing, they had a poor mental attitude toward one another, as we have seen. For another, they had a poor mental attitude toward Paul. They accused him of talking big but being little. They flung out the accusation that Paul walked "according to the flesh" (2 Corinthians 10:2b), that is, in a carnal manner.

Paul's reply to the Corinthians' accusation

demonstrates just how actively the devil was battling for the Corinthians' minds and is battling for our minds today. He explains in verses 4 and 5 that the devil works through anti-Christian philosophies (he calls these "imaginations") and unscriptural concepts which oppose right thinking about God. In other words, the devil launches strategic attacks against us to prevent us from forming a proper concept of what God is like.

In his book *Your God Is Too Small*, J. B. Phillips does a beautiful job of identifying the inadequate concepts of God which many of us have. He mentions the idea of God being "the Resident Policeman," who is always looking over our shoulder, ready to slap our hands when we do wrong. Then there's the view of God, "the Meek and Mild." Also, there's the concept of God as "the Grand Old Man." He includes, too, the picture of God as "the Managing Director," plus many more weak views of God. His main thrust is intended to show how the devil uses strategy to bring God down and to pump up the human ego.

You can see this in Genesis 3, when the devil attacked Eve's concept of God. He knew that it wouldn't be very smart to come up to Eve and deny the truthfulness of God as the first point of attack. So he decided to get her to question God's goodness. He told Eve, in effect, "You know, Eve, God's withholding something from you. Isn't he? Would a good God restrict your rights by placing one of the trees of the garden off limits?"

Doesn't the devil's line remind you of Dewey's

permissiveness in child-rearing and education? You know how it goes. "You mean to tell me that as a parent you withhold something from your child? You don't give him everything he wants? How unkind of you!"

"Eve," the devil seemed to reason, "do you mean to tell me that God is holding something back from you? Is it possible that the thing he's holding back is something that would be good for you? How can he be so mean as to deprive you of something good?"

And so the devil worked away at Eve's thinking until he got her mind firmly in his clutches. He got her thinking his thoughts. And once that had happened she started adding to what God had said. Her concept of God got all twisted.

You may wonder why God prohibited Adam and Eve from eating of the tree of the knowledge of good and evil. The answer is: he needed a point of testing. And didn't he make the test simple? Just one tree was off limits. If I had the assignment to figure out an appropriate test, likely I would have placed at least fifteen trees in the garden and ordered: "Don't taste that one! Stay away from that one! Don't touch that one!" But God is so gracious; he put just one tree off limits.

Something else. God put the emphasis on the positive. It was as though he said to our first parents, "You can eat of *every* tree except one, just one. You can enjoy this beautiful, perfect garden to your hearts' content. But I have hung a *No Trespassing* sign on just one tree to test your obedience. You see, I don't want you to be robots. I want you to love me by choice."

Now, please, don't think there was something clandestine about the fruit of the tree, something sinisterly intriguing. I see a ridiculous advertisement once in awhile for cranapple juice. It shows a half-clad gal among some leaves, picking an apple. I guess she's supposed to represent Eve reaching for the forbidden fruit. The ad almost has her saying, "Mm, mmm, good! Boy, oh boy, if I can just eat that apple. It's got some powerful secrets in it."

Nonsense! God's restriction had nothing to do with the fruit of the tree. There was nothing wrong with the fruit. God made it. The tree served as a point of testing. That's all. He could have put the same restriction on any of the trees in the garden. But he picked the tree of the knowledge of good and evil and commanded, "Don't eat of it!"

But the more Eve looked at that tree, and the more she thought the devil's thoughts, the lower her estimation of God became. She began to attribute things to God that were not worthy of God. She figured God was neither good nor fair. That made the devil bolder than before. He became so bold, in fact, that he accused God of lying. Genesis 3:4 captures the scene: "And the serpent said unto the woman, Ye shall not surely die."

The devil's assault on Eve's thought life continued until she saw that the tree's fruit was good to eat, nice-looking, and "to be desired to make one wise" (verse 6). Remember? Sins don't happen in a moment. You don't fall in a moment. The devil may spend hours, days, weeks, months, and even years preparing you for a fall. He plants subtle stimuli in your thinking until he has you preconditioned for a fall. Then he strikes. He certainly spent enough time on Eve to get her to take the bait; then the trap slammed shut. She grabbed the fruit and gave some of it to her husband. And the idiot—he ate of it right along with her.

Let me digress a bit to point out that Adam should have been some kind of help to Eve as her spiritual leader, but he was no help at all. Often I speak to women's groups about the role of women. Invariably a woman will approach me after the meeting in response to 1 Corinthians 14:35, which advises that if a woman wants to learn anything, she should ask her husband at home. Her complaint is, "Why should I ask my husband? He wouldn't know anything about the Bible."

The same thing shows up in a Sunday school class. I can ask questions, and all the women raise their hands for a chance to answer. They've been in a Bible study fellowship somewhere, and they have learned a commendable lot about the Bible. Meanwhile, their husbands sit in the class with a blank stare and listen to their wives' answers.

What do I recommend? Just this—Christian men need to get with it. They need to start learning something about God's Word so they can be the spiritual leaders God expects them to be. God's job description for a husband includes nurturing and cherishing his wife in spiritual things. It isn't the wife's job to nurture and cherish her husband in such things. And God expects a Christian father to bring up the children in the nurture and admonition of the Lord. It's tragic that we have men in our churches who are illiterate regarding the Scriptures. So I insist—Christian men need to get with it.

Let me remind you—the devil's top strategy in the battle for your mind is to lower your concept of God. He lowered Eve's concept of God, and the consequences speak for themselves. Don't make the mistake of thinking you can outsmart the devil, because you don't have a ghost of a chance of winning. The day you think you can outsmart him, you'll get the surprise of your life; he will knock you out of the contest in the first round. There's only one hope for you: fill your mind with a concept of the triune God as the Scriptures portray him. The truth of God establishes our vision, straightens our course, and resets our compass on the North Pole of accurate thought.

Sacred strategy 6

A soldier going into battle must know his enemy. He must also know what kinds of attacks the enemy is likely to launch. And he most certainly needs to know what resources are available to him for defeating the enemy. The same things apply to the Christian soldier. He must recognize that the devil is his lifelong enemy. He must understand that the devil masterminds numerous attacks, many of which are sneak attacks using the subtle stimuli of an ungodly world system. And he must know the resources available to him for defeating the enemy.

Before our Lord went to the cross to die for us, he held briefing sessions with his disciples so that they might understand how to resist the devil and be the kind of men God wanted them to be. One of those sessions included the teaching in John 15 and 16 about the believer's resources in God the Father, God the Son, and God the Holy Spirit. As I study this teaching and related Scriptures, I get a clear picture of the part each member of the Trinity plays in helping me to resist the devil's assault on my thinking.

John 15 introduces me to the first resource I have—God the Father. Jesus says in verse 1: "I am the true vine, and my Father is the husbandman." Some time ago, when I stayed in the home of an eighty-six-year-old California grape producer, I got a better appreciation of what it means that my heavenly Father is the "husbandman," the vinedresser. My host took me on a really interesting tour of his vineyards. As we walked along, he pointed out different kinds of grapes and explained how their vines had to be trimmed. Different vines demanded different trimming. I learned that it takes a lot of knowledge plus a lot of work on the part of a vinedresser to get grapes he's proud of.

No wonder my vines back home weren't producing grapes. I just cut them where I thought it would make the vines look nice. So the tour in California taught me a lot—about agriculture and the meaning of John 15. Now I look at Jesus' teaching in John 15 that my heavenly Father is the vinedresser and I'm a branch in the vine, and I think about how much personal care the Father invests in me. And I think about how much he knows about me, which is *everything*—my past, my present, and my future. Nothing I have done, am doing, or will do takes him by surprise. There can never be a time when it's three o'clock in the afternoon and he is sitting in Heaven and complains, "Oh, my land, I just got a phone call from Earl Radmacher. You know what that dope did? If I'd only known what a loser he is, I never would have brought him into my family." Instead, my Father in Heaven takes care of me. He is the vinedresser, and he works on me, a branch, to make me productive.

Jesus tells us in John 15:2 that the Father takes away every branch that doesn't bear fruit. This doesn't mean he jerks the branch out of the vine and throws it away. A recent tour of the vineyards in Israel near Hebron shed great light on this. Traveling past those vineyards, I noticed that the vines in one field were tied up to wires suspended from poles, whereas the vines in the field immediately adjacent were down on the ground. You see, the vinedressers were preparing their vines for the new season of productivity. Thus, they picked up the vines from the ground and attached them to wires where they would not be contaminated by the dirt. Also, there on the wires they would be open to receive the light of the sun.

I have since learned that the grapes are highly susceptible to contamination from the dirt. How fitting it is, then, to note that the neat thing the Father does is to "purge" what has already borne fruit. To "purge" is not simply to prune but to cleanse, as is noted by the repetition of the same root Greek word in verse 3: "Now ye are _clean_ through the word which I have spoken unto you."

The Word, then, is the implement God the

Father uses to cleanse me. He takes his love, omnipotence, and omniscience, and he puts them to work through the Word to shape me up so that I will bear fruit. That sure does something for my Christian living to know I have that kind of heavenly Father—that he is working in me. It helps me to produce, knowing that he is so powerful that the devil can't do a thing without my Father allowing him to do it. This knowledge of God the Father fortifies me. It is a weapon I can use in my battles with the devil for the control of my thinking.

The second resource I have for combating the devil is the Son of God, Jesus Christ. The Father is the pruner, the purger, the vinedresser; but Jesus Christ, too, is doing something for me. From Hebrews 7:25 I learn that he is presently at the right hand of the Father in Heaven. He told the disciples in John 16 that he would leave them in order to return to the Father. There you find him explaining, "It is expedient for you that I go away" (verse 7). Why was his return to the Father expedient? Jesus explained further, "If I go not away, the Comforter will not come unto you; but if I depart, I will send him unto you" (verse 7b). Then Jesus continued by saying in effect, "What will I do when I am with the Father? I will be your defense attorney up there. I will be your advocate, and not one case the devil brings against you will stick."

First John 2:1 tells me that Jesus Christ kept his word. He is in Heaven now, pleading my case whenever the devil brings an accusation against me. The Apostle John puts it this way: "My little children, these things write I unto you, that ye sin not. And if any man sin, we have an advocate with the Father, Jesus Christ the righteous."

Hebrews 7:25 emphasizes further that Jesus Christ "ever liveth to make intercession" for us Christians. This means right now he is in Heaven praying for me and for you. He never stops praying for us. And because he is infinite, his praying for me doesn't take any time away from his praying for you and every other Christian. That's a little tough for me to grab hold of, because I find that when I'm praying for one thing it takes time from other things. Fortunately, he doesn't have the problem of time. As C. S. Lewis observed: "He is able to give all of himself to everybody all the time." What a resource we have in the Son of God for our battles against the devil!

Now, look again at what Jesus says in John 16. He has already said that he must go away, but he will send the Comforter to his followers. Then, in verse 13, he promises, "Howbeit when he, the Spirit of truth, is come, he will guide you into all truth." All of this tells me I have still another resource for battling Satan. That resource is God the Holy Spirit, who lives in me to fill my thoughts with the truth—the Word of God.

The battle lines are drawn pretty tight, aren't they? Satan, the god of this world system, assaults my thinking with stimuli which are designed to pull me down and make me ineffective for God, and the

Holy Spirit desires to guide me into the truth—to help me to think straight about God and his will so that I may be effective as a Christian. Paul, knowing about all of this, writes in 2 Corinthians 10:5 that I should be "bringing into captivity every thought to the obedience of Christ."

How am I going to do what Paul directs me to do—bring not just some thoughts but *every* thought into obedience to Christ? One thing for sure—I can't do it unless I know the Word of God. If I don't have the grid of Scripture built in over my mind and heart, I'm sunk. But with the grid of Scripture over my mind and heart, I can test the thoughts that are coming, and I can decide which thoughts I ought to allow to settle in my inner self and which thoughts I ought to throw out. Putting it another way, the grid of Scripture shows me which thoughts are worthy of God and which thoughts are not worthy of God. And it is the Holy Spirit who helps me to build that all-important grid.

We hear a great deal today about the filling of the Spirit. Perhaps you are aware of the fact that a better word for "filling" is *control*. So we exhort Christians to be controlled by the Spirit; that is, let the Holy Spirit take control of their thought processes so that they will do those things which demonstrate obedience to Jesus Christ. I regard this control by the Holy Spirit to be extremely significant, for I am going to be influenced by the satanic world system unless I yield to the Spirit's control of my thought life.

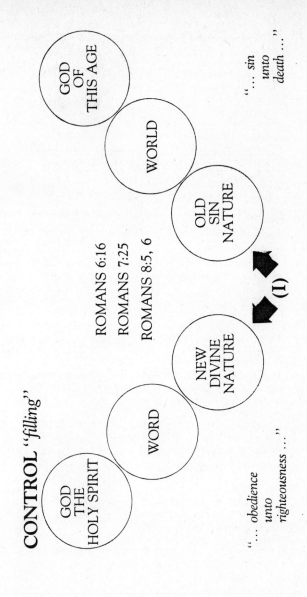

CONTROL *"filling"*

GOD THE HOLY SPIRIT

WORD

NEW DIVINE NATURE

"... obedience unto righteousness ...."

ROMANS 6:16
ROMANS 7:25
ROMANS 8:5, 6

(I)

GOD OF THIS AGE

WORLD

OLD SIN NATURE

"... sin unto death ...."

When you and I were born into this world, each of us was born with a sin nature. Ephesians 2:3 says we "were by nature the children of wrath." The sin nature is energized by Satan—the god of this age—who works through the world system—the cosmos—to get me to do his will. As the head of that hierarchical system, the devil has probably countless millions of demons carrying out his orders in the unseen world. If I do his will, the result is going to be sin unto death—separation from the resources I have in God. When I am living in sin, you see, I am living in separation from the infinite resources of God which are available for life in Christ.

On the other hand, when I came to know Jesus Christ as Savior and Lord I was born again, and I received a new nature—a divine nature. (See John 3:3-6; 2 Corinthians 5:17; 2 Peter 1:4.) I received a new capacity through which the Holy Spirit can work to get me to do the will of God. He works through the Word of God—the Truth—influencing my new nature so that the result will be obedience unto righteousness.

I have, then, the ability to take every one of my thoughts and actions, line them up in order, and attribute every one of them ultimately to either God or Satan. Not necessarily directly, but either directly or indirectly, either voluntarily or involuntarily, either consciously or unconsciously. Nothing in this context is neutral, because everything I do is a response either to the energy of the god of this age or to the Spirit of God.

Some persons get real upset when I say something is of the devil. "Wait a minute," they object, "that's kind of strong."

I reply, "Well, would you say it's of God?"

"Uh ... uh ... I really can't say that it's of God," they admit.

Then I question, "If it isn't of the devil and it isn't of God, who is it of?"

The usual response is, "It must be of the flesh."

The problem with that answer is, the flesh is not a *who*. The flesh is the sin nature through which a *who* works, and the *who* is the devil himself. He is the energizer, who works through his hierarchy of demons to appeal to me through the world system by means of my sin nature to get me to do his will.

This is why I say life actions are being performed as the result of my thinking. And that thinking either fits God's thinking or the devil's thinking. It takes the Word of God to help me distinguish between the two kinds. And it is the Holy Spirit who teaches me the Word.

Let me review the steps for bringing into captivity every thought to the obedience of Christ. 1) Fill your thinking with a scriptural view of what God is like. 2) Obey the Word. "Yield ... your members as instruments of righteousness unto God" (Romans 6:13). Keep on rejecting wrong attitudes and crooked thoughts by maintaining the grid of Scripture over your mind and heart. These steps will guide you to victory over Satan, for you will be availing yourself of the all-powerful resources of the triune God.

Right thinking about who owns the church 7

Now we are ready to practice the process of right thinking that we have produced in the previous chapters. And the best place to start thinking right is with the church, the family of believers God has given us for developing our potential in Christ.

You may think there are quite a few critics of the church today, but the fact is there have always been critics of the church. For example, in the 1910 Lyman Beecher lectures at Yale, a number of references appear as evidence that the church was under attack back then. One comment indicated, "The church has to many Christians become an object to apologize for, and has ceased to be an institution to be sacrificed for and loved."

The speaker who made this comment went on to say, "The effect of this widespread skepticism in regard to the church is manifesting itself increasingly." He described the church's chief critics as "the people who write newspaper articles on 'the decadence of the pulpit,' who publish novels showing that if Christlike people desire to accomplish anything worthwhile, they must cut loose from the church, who deliver lectures in which the most sparkling paragraphs are gibes at the preachers and thrusts at the church members."

The 1950s and 60s, of course, were full of critics of the church. Interestingly, most of them were Protestant ministers. A 1968 *Christianity Today* editorial, "Crepe-Hangers in the Church," referred to what some of the critics had written:

"Five out of every six church buildings in America could be sold and dismantled without damage to the Christian mission."

"The local church is no longer a satisfactory vehicle for doing the work of Christ."

"The traditional work of the local parish ... is hardly likely to survive in an era of religious revolution."

"The Christian ministry is doomed to disappear with the bourgeois culture that made room for it."

The year 1971 wasn't such a great year for the church's popularity either. *Presbyterian Life* carried an article, "College Students Talk about Religion," in which James Hoffman observed, "I can conceive a time in my lifetime when there will be no need for churches. People will find other ways to meet spiritual needs."

A more positive view came into focus, however, with the publishing of Findley Edge's book *The Greening of the Church.* And one of the best books I have read on the church is the recently published *God's Forgetful Pilgrims* by Michael Griffiths. Also, it is good to see more and more young people developing a healthy respect for the church. So I'm optimistic about the church's future.

This doesn't mean, of course, that we ought to go into a cheerleading routine in front of every building having a church name attached to it. The fact is, not every church deserves the Good Churchkeeping Seal of Approval. You see, many edifices called churches are not churches at all in the biblical sense, just as many individuals calling themselves Christians are not really Christians. There are many substitutes for the real thing. My book *The Nature of the Church* (Western Baptist Press) deals at length with the subject of what a true church is, but here I shall deal with this subject briefly because I feel strongly that we need to be sensitive to this question.

Let me illustrate this point.

A young man is walking along downtown when his attention is captured by a most attractive young woman in the show window of a fashionable department store. She is beautifully dressed and her beauty is enhanced by exquisite jewelry and tastefully applied cosmetics. The young man walks up to the window, admires the young woman for awhile, and decides that he must make her acquaintance. So he steps into the store, goes through the door that leads into the show window, introduces himself to the young woman, and asks her for a date. But to his astonishment, she does not respond in any way to his request. She doesn't say "yes," she doesn't say "no." She doesn't even blush! Then it dawns on him that she can't respond because she is not a young woman at all; she is a mannequin. He leaves the store and continues his walk, mumbling to himself, "She looked like a beautiful young woman. She dressed like a beautiful young woman. But she wasn't the real thing."

From a distance some things look like churches. They dress like churches. They have signs on them like churches. But a closer examination shows that they are not churches at all. They are simply religious organizations.

The Word of God makes it clear that there are certain prerequisites for a church to qualify as the real thing. To simply hang a church sign on the front of a building to announce, FIRST CHURCH, doesn't make it a church. Also, all churches shouldn't be judged on the basis of the counterfeits that call themselves churches. We must distinguish between what the Bible calls *the* church and organizations which are churches.

The church—the church of Jesus Christ—includes all who have placed their faith in the Son of God as their substitute, believing that he died for them on the cross. Regardless of their denominational preference, they belong to the church of Jesus Christ; and because I am a believer in the Son of God, I am related to them. We are all one in Christ. Granted, some may choose certain kinds of unscriptural relationships which hinder our fellowship, but the fact remains we are one in Christ even though that oneness is not always expressed.

So there is only one church that may properly be called *the* church of Jesus Christ or the body of Christ. But down through the centuries that church has been manifested through organizations known as local churches. These local churches ought to reflect the character of *the* church. In other words, each local church is a microcosm of the body of Christ, which is the macrocosm. Nothing should exist in a local church that is contradictory to the character of the body of Christ. When a local church ceases to be a justifiable representation of *the* church, it ceases to be a local church. A church that does not honor Jesus Christ as Lord—perfect God and perfect Man—and the Bible as God's revelation—our only rule of faith and practice—is merely a religious organization. It is not a church.

If you are a Christian, you are responsible to join and support a local church. And, of course, you should be vitally related to a local church that is a mission force, not a mission field. Some Christians purposely join a church on the basis of whether it looks like a mission field. They reason that they will have a great time winning its unregenerate members to Christ. That's wrong, for a mission field isn't a church. You need to unite with a church that is a mission force, ready to act as a thrust behind you to help you reach mission fields. We must, then, be aware of the difference between what is truly *church* and what is counterfeit.

Having clarified our definition of "church," let's examine what is right about it. The most important thing is that it belongs to Jesus Christ. I find it interesting to hear some persons criticize the church and suggest giving it away when they don't own it in the first place. I have no right to give away something that belongs to someone else; and no one has the right to give away the church—it belongs to God's Son.

Jesus Christ, who owns the church, instituted the church. Matthew 16 carries the story. The Lord Jesus had asked his disciples that all-important question: "Whom say ye that I am?" Peter was quick to confess, "Thou art the Christ, the Son of the living God." Now Jesus Christ responds to Peter's confession with the startling declaration of how he planned to use the big fisherman. He reveals: "Thou art Peter, and upon this rock I will build my church; and the gates of hell shall not prevail against it" (verse 18).

I don't see any need to separate Peter from his confession. Some persons get real upset about calling Peter the rock on which Christ was going to build his church. As far as I'm concerned, Peter was the rock, the one upon whom Christ planned to build his church along with the other apostles. Nor do I see any reason to get upset over our Lord's promise to give Peter "the keys of the kingdom of heaven" (verse 19).

As I see it, a key is used for opening something.

Peter opened something vitally related to the church. What was it? On the Day of Pentecost Peter opened up the message of the gospel to the international delegation of Jews who were in Jerusalem to observe the Feast of Pentecost. And wasn't it Peter who later visited Samaria to authenticate what was taking place there as believers preached the gospel? Also, you may recall, it was Peter who went to the home of Cornelius, a Gentile, and opened the door of salvation to him by declaring the gospel. It was during Peter's visit to Cornelius that he made the startling remark, "Of a truth I perceive that God is no respecter of persons" (Acts 10:34).

Put it all together. Peter was used of the Lord to open the door to the gospel for the Jews, for the Samaritans, and for the Gentiles. Who was left? Nobody! All the doors were opened. Peter had used the keys. So, now, who cares who has the keys, for there are no more locked doors.

Jesus Christ had informed Peter, "I'm going to build something different, a church, an *ekklesia*—an assembly of called-out people. And, Peter, you're going to serve as part of the foundation." Later the Apostle Paul identified the apostles and prophets as part of the foundation, Jesus Christ as the chief cornerstone, and evangelists and pastors-teachers as builders of the superstructure (Ephesians 2:20; 4:11, 12).

Actually, the concept of an *ekklesia,* an assembly, was fairly well known in Peter's day, for the word applied to a number of gatherings in

Greek society. When the citizens of a city-state gathered together in a legislative meeting, they called their assembly an *ekklesia.* As far back as the Old Testament age, the Jews were accustomed to all kinds of *ekklesias.* They had assemblies of military men, assemblies of judges, the assembly of Israel, and there was also the concept of assemblies of evildoers. So Jesus' declaration to Peter that he was going to build an assembly wasn't completely out of the range of Peter's understanding.

Now examine Jesus' prediction more closely. He was telling Peter: "Peter, I'm going to build an assembly, but it's going to be unique. First of all, it's going to belong to me. I plan to build *my ekklesia.* It will be mine personally, founded upon my blood, my sacrifice. Furthermore, my *ekklesia* will never die. The gates of death, the gates of Hell shall never prevail against my *ekklesia,* my church. You can count on it, Peter. My church will have perpetuity; it will survive as my personal object."

So when people talk about the death of the church, they must not be talking about the institution—the *ekklesia*—Jesus started, for his church will never die. At the Rapture, when the Lord comes for the church, there's going to be a church. He is not coming to receive nothing; he is coming to receive something. And that something is his church which he has built on earth by his power and through his servants.

The church, then, was started by Jesus Christ and is being perpetuated by him. It belongs to him.

In the second chapter of Acts, we come upon the first local manifestation of the church which our Lord promised to build. The stage for it had been set by the promise and provision of the Lord Jesus Christ. It sprang into existence as Peter preached the gospel on the Day of Pentecost. According to verse 41, 3,000 persons believed what Peter proclaimed about Christ, were baptized and introduced into an *ekklesia*—a church. And what a church it was! Its members continued steadfastly in the apostles' doctrine, in fellowship, in the breaking of bread, and in prayer (verse 42). The results of such faithfulness to the Lord were joy, sharing together, favor with all the people, and best of all—"the Lord was adding to the church daily such as should be saved" (verse 47b). So what Christ prophesied in Matthew 16:18 as a future project had its concrete, historical reality in the second chapter of Acts. And the Lord added daily to that church. Jesus Christ, as Head of the church, was vitally and personally involved in building his church.

That was the First Church of Jerusalem, and it became instrumental in the founding of other churches as its members fanned out across continents to preach and teach Jesus Christ. Even the ministry of the Apostle Paul had its roots in the Jerusalem church, for one of its members—Stephen—witnessed a good confession before Paul in Paul's preconversion days (see Acts 7:54-60). Stephen's faithfulness to Christ in the face of intense opposition apparently stabbed

Paul's conscience and prepared him for his dramatic meeting with Christ on the Damascus Road. Paul became a believer and a missionary, and God used him to found what Paul called "the churches of Christ" (Romans 16:16).

That's significant, isn't it? *The churches of Christ.* Paul's reference is plural. He's talking about a number of live, visible, local representations of the body of Christ, and he indicates they all belong to Jesus Christ. Undoubtedly each church had specific problems, but there was something absolutely right with all of them—they were Christ's personal property.

You find the same emphasis in Paul's letters to the church at Thessalonica. It was a church that was owned lock, stock, and barrel by Jesus Christ (1 Thessalonians 1:1; 2 Thessalonians 1:1).

Even the church at Corinth had a divine ownership (2 Corinthians 1:1). Sure there was a lot that was wrong in the Corinthian church, but there were some things that were right. The church honored Jesus Christ as Lord, both divine and human. They honored the Word of God as the final revelation from God. And although the members displayed an immaturity and a carnal attitude, there was nonetheless a solid basis for identifying the Corinthian church as a bona fide church.

Finally, in Revelation 2 and 3, John the Apostle records the Lord's evaluation of each of seven churches in Asia Minor. As you read what the Lord said to and about each of these churches, you can't fail to observe that each belonged to Christ and was directly responsible to him. He demonstrated his right to scrutinize and mobilize those seven churches because they were his churches.

Yes, even the seventh of those churches—the church at Laodicea—belonged to Jesus Christ. But it was on the verge of going out of business. Our Lord warned that he was about to remove its candlestick because of its atrociously poor spiritual condition.

The Laodicean condition tells us something, doesn't it? It tells us that we have no right to tamper with our Lord's churches. They are not ours to give away. They are his to do with as he pleases. Furthermore, it tells us that when a church no longer shines as a light for Christ, it ceases to exist as a church. It has become simply a religious organization.

So the next time you hear someone knock a true church, remind him that he is criticizing the greatest institution going—an institution which belongs to Jesus Christ himself. And that is something that is very right about the church!

Right thinking about who lives in the church 8

Once in awhile we learn about a deadlock between some old fellow and the authorities over the old fellow's property. His house sits in the middle of a proposed superhighway or on land the city wants to turn into a public golf course, or it is the last house to be razed in an urban renewal project. At any rate, he refuses to leave the old homestead and the authorities refuse to let him stay. Eventually a bulldozer takes up a threatening position four or five feet from the house while the old fellow mans a defensive position on his front porch—in a rocking chair, shotgun in hand and hound dog at his side. Of course the whole episode ends with the old fellow as the loser, proving once again that "you can't fight city hall."

Any critics of the church who want to bulldoze it away in order to prepare the ground for some new kind of Christian representation might as well save themselves the trouble, because the church is here to stay. Rather than confronting an old fellow with a shotgun and a hound dog, they face an invincible resident when they try to dispose of the church. The Holy Spirit is that resident, and he will never abandon the property.

Keeping in mind the fact that *the* church of Jesus Christ consists of born-again persons, consider the Apostle Paul's emphasis on the Spirit's residence in the church. There's Ephesians 2:19-22, for example: "Now therefore ye are no more strangers and foreigners, but fellowcitizens with the saints, and of the household of God; and are built upon the foundation of the apostles and prophets, Jesus Christ himself being the chief corner stone. In whom all the building fitly framed together groweth unto an holy temple in the Lord; in whom ye also are built together for an habitation of God through the Spirit." In this passage the apostle is looking at the church in its broadest perspective. He sees it as the universal church, the body of Christ. And he identifies it as the dwelling place of God through his Spirit. It is the place where God manifests himself on earth.

In 1 Corinthians 3:16, 17 Paul says pretty much the same thing. But here he has the local church in view as God's dwelling place. If you take the time to read the preceding verses of the third chapter of 1 Corinthians, you will learn why he introduces the thought that the local church is occupied by God. Paul had laid the foundation for the church at Corinth. Jesus Christ was the foundation. Others had come along to take leadership roles in the church—to build on the foundation.

And Paul sounds a note of caution about how the construction job was to be handled. Only the best materials were to be used: "gold, silver, precious stones." Cheap materials—"wood, hay, stubble"—were to be avoided. In other words, the Lord's ministers were to work faithfully for the good of the church, for the Lord would hold each worker accountable for any damage done to the church. Paul comments: "Know ye not that ye are the temple of God, and that the Spirit of God dwelleth in you? If any man defile the temple of God, him shall God destroy; for the temple of God is holy, which temple ye are."

The Greek text omits the definite article "the" before the word "temple" in this passage, because it would be wrong to call any local church *the* temple of God. That designation is reserved exclusively for the total body of Christ. The absence of the definite article suggests that Paul wanted to emphasize the character of the Corinthian church. Its members were of the same character, or quality, as *the* body of Christ. They were "temple of God," for the Holy Spirit was living in them. They were the place where God was manifesting himself.

A. T. Robertson, that excellent Greek scholar of another day, rendered the first part of 1 Corinthians 3:17 as "church wreckers God will wreck." Not a bad translation. God warns that he will deal a serious blow to those who are out to wreck a local church.

So the universal church is God's dwelling place, and the local church is his dwelling place too. But—and this is a startling fact—individual Christians are also his dwelling place. Paul hands us this important information in 1 Corinthians 6:19: "What? Know ye not that your body is the temple of the Holy Ghost which is in you, which ye have of God, and ye are not your own?"

Here's something else that's important to know: the individual believer's body is an extremely expensive bit of real estate, for Paul tells us that it was bought with a price, a price he discloses in Ephesians 1:7, 14 as the blood of Christ. No wonder he challenges the believer to "glorify God in your body ..." (1 Corinthians 6:20). Such a high-priced residence should accommodate the owner's every wish and purpose.

In Old Testament times God didn't dwell like this in his people. Instead, he manifested himself in the Tabernacle and in the Temple. It is only in the Church Age that he lives in Christians as his temple. And it is important to recognize that he calls us Christians his temple, and doesn't call a building his temple. Getting hold of this truth can help us maintain a desire to keep his temple clean.

Another way of saying we are God's temple is to say we are his sanctuary. Often we call the central place of worship the sanctuary, but we aren't accurate in doing so. Occasionally you will enter a place of worship and notice a sign announcing: *You are entering the sanctuary; please be quiet.* I take issue with a sign like that, and I have engaged quite a few pastors in conversation about it.

"Pastor," I have said, "I just want to bring to your attention the fact that when I came through that door—the one with the sign—I didn't come into the sanctuary; the sanctuary came into the auditorium."

The point is—by God's grace I am his sanctuary. A room is not his sanctuary. God doesn't reside in a building; he resides in his people. I must admit, though, calling the room we worship in the "auditorium" may not be such a hot idea either. I used to like to call it the auditorium until someone asked me, "Do you know the derivation of *auditorium?*" When I confessed that I didn't, he clued me in. "It comes from *audio,* meaning 'to hear,' and *toro,* meaning 'the bull.' So it is literally 'the place where you hear the bull.'"

When I was a member of a church during my college days, I had an interesting conversation one Sunday morning with an elder of the church, who was a good friend. We were standing on the church steps, about to enter the building. The elder was finishing a last cigarette before church.

I asked, "Why don't we go in? We're late, you know."

He replied, "I'd like to finish this smoke first. You go in, and I'll be there in a minute or so."

I asked, "Why don't you take your cigarette with you and go in now?"

He gave me a strange look and demanded, "Take this cigarette in there? Don't you know that our church is the temple of God?"

I offered, "That isn't the way I understand it. As I see it, you have that thing sticking in the temple of God right now!"

That was the last time he smoked a cigarette.

Now, I don't think he'll get to wear a gold medal on his chest in Heaven because he quit smoking, but it is certainly commendable that he dealt with an important principle—a Christian's body is God's dwelling place and ought to be kept holy for his purposes.

Romans 12:1 indicates that every believer should present his body to God as a living sacrifice. Why? For God's use in manifesting himself on earth. Therefore, a believer should not do anything with his body that will detract from being a holy temple of God.

Yes, this means that there are some things I don't do. Not because God will love me more because I don't do them (he couldn't love me any more than he loves me in Christ), but because I love him enough to try to keep his residence on earth clean.

When I was a seminary student, my brother sent me a beautiful leather briefcase with my name inscribed on it in gold. It made me feel great to carry that briefcase around.

One day I got word that my brother was coming to visit me. As I anticipated his coming, a kooky kind of thought entered my head. I thought, Wouldn't it be interesting if my brother arrived and found me walking down the driveway to the garbage cans with the leather briefcase full of garbage—tin cans, potato peelings, paper boxes, coffee grounds, and the previous semester's term papers crammed into the beautiful briefcase?

I want to assure you—if my brother had caught me in a situation like that, he would have been far more concerned about the condition of my brain than the condition of the briefcase he'd given me.

Your body wasn't given to you by a wonderful Creator for you to use as a garbage can. It belongs to him for his tremendous, holy purposes. And since he lives in your body, you will want to be extremely careful about what enters your body through the eye gate and ear gate, about what your mouth says, about what your hands grab and where your feet go.

You are a temple of God on earth.

Right thinking about who runs the church 9

It happened on a Sunday evening around Halloween, according to a certain story. Some mischievous youths decided to inject high intensity excitement into the preaching service of the local First Church of the Hoot 'N Hollers. So they outfitted one of their guys with a devil's costume, complete with horns, pointed tail, hooves, and pitchfork. Then they hid among the shrubs outside the church and waited for the mood of the highly emotional congregation to rise to a fever pitch.

The moment they waited for came. The preacher was concluding his fire and brimstone message. Members of the congregation were shrieking and shaking with emotion. So the pranksters gave the signal for the "devil" to burst into the service.

Seeing the "devil" come down the center aisle was too much for the frenzied crowd. They headed for the exits as fast as they could go. But one of their number couldn't make it to safety. Being heavily endowed with adipose tissue, particularly around her posterior, she got wedged between two pews. Realizing her predicament, she pointed at the "devil" and ordered, "Stay right where you are, Mr. Devil. Don't take another step. I'll have you know I've been a member of this church for thirty-four years. And I've been on your side the whole time!"

There's no denying most churches have their share of members who have been on the devil's side for a long time, and this has undoubtedly given critics of the church all the more reason to write the church off as a bad deal. But for every hypocrite in the church there are hundreds of genuine Christians who are concerned about fitting into God's program.

And God does have a program for the church, a wonderful plan of operation which he superintends. It involves church government and a variety of gifts. These two facets of his plan— government and gifts—kept in proper perspective, will guarantee that a local church will function efficiently as a manifestation of God on earth.

It is important to get hold of this concept of a local church, for there are quite a few persons who claim they don't need the church. "I listen to several religious broadcasts every Sunday, and get all the church I need." "I have my Bible study group, so I don't need the church." Have you heard comments like these? Is there any support for such reasoning?

The church is not a religious broadcast, nor a

series of such broadcasts. It is not a Bible study group either. A church is an organization based on the teaching of God's Word. Its members have banded themselves together as obedient believers in Jesus Christ for fellowship, worship, and service. In doing so, they have voluntarily submitted themselves to spiritual leadership which the New Testament identifies as elders or bishops (1 Timothy 3:1-7; Titus 1:5-9) and deacons (1 Timothy 3:8-13; Philippians 1:1).

Every believer should be vitally related to a local church, for sheep without a shepherd go astray. In the New Testament, believers in Jesus Christ were related to a local manifestation of the body of Christ and were in submission to God's appointed leadership. Hebrews 13:7 underscores the importance of this kind of relationship: "Remember them which have the rule over you, who have spoken unto you the word of God: whose faith follow, considering the end of their conversation [manner of life]." And verse 17 comes at it again: "Obey them that have the rule over you, and submit yourselves: for they watch for your souls, as they that must give account, that they may do it with joy, and not with grief: for that is unprofitable for you."

Is a Christian under obligation, then, to digest everything a pastor-teacher says without chewing it first to see whether it is worth swallowing? No. According to God's plan for the church, every Christian is a believer-priest and has the responsibility to see to it that his spiritual leaders, including the pastor, are maintaining the doctrine of God's Word. If a spiritual leader ceases to be faithful to the Scriptures, the believers—two or three at least—are supposed to bring their accusation before the assembly; and the assembly is supposed to decide the issue (1 Timothy 5:19, 20; see also Matthew 18:15-17).

Various references in the Pauline epistles spotlight the importance of church organization. In Titus 1:5 Paul instructed Titus, a pastor, to "set in order" the things that were lacking in the church on the island of Crete. When the apostle corresponded with the church at Colosse he announced, "I am with you in the spirit, joying and beholding your order, and the stedfastness of your faith in Christ" (Colossians 2:5). Interestingly, the word he used for "order" is *taxin*, meaning a "most precise and exact order."

In his book *Oneness with Christ: Popular Studies in the Epistle to the Colossians*, W. R. Nicholson comments that *taxin* suggests "each one in his place, submissive to discipline, submissive to them that are over them in the Lord, no self-will, no isolated action.... Order and faith are thus united, and the provision of either without the other marks an unprosperous church, for in that case the one becomes formalism and the other fanaticism."

Paul's epistles reveal further that there were local church officers (1 Timothy 3:1-16; Titus 1:5-9) and church rolls, at least for the widows who were to receive help (1 Timothy 5:9).

Evidence seems to support the fact that there were carefully kept membership records. The numbers were known (Acts 2:41; 4:4), and church discipline assumes that members could be removed from a church roll (1 Corinthians 5:13). There were rules for orderly procedures and practices in the churches (1 Corinthians 11:1-34; 14:1-40), including a procedure for handling church finances (1 Corinthians 16:2).

It is clear, then, that God wants every local church to function "decently and in order" (1 Corinthians 14:40), maintaining a proper balance of faith and action so that it will be a credible manifestation of God on earth.

But God has not left the implementation of his plan to human ingenuity and aptitude. As a counterpart to government he has bestowed *gifts* upon every member of the church, so that every person in the body of Christ has something to do and can do it effectively. The Apostle Peter underscores this fact in 1 Peter 4:10, 11: "As every man hath received the gift, even so minister the same one to another, as good stewards of the manifold grace of God. If any man speak, let him speak as the oracles of God; if any man minister, let him do it as of the ability which God giveth: that God in all things may be glorified through Jesus Christ, to whom be praise and dominion for ever and ever. Amen." The Apostle Paul, too, stressed this same truth in Romans 12:1-8; Ephesians 4:1-16; and 1 Corinthians 12—14).

As a matter of fact, one reason why Paul wrote his first letter to the Corinthians was to explain the subject of the distribution and implementation of the spiritual gifts. You probably recall how the Corinthian church was fragmented, factious, and frustrated. Its members lined up behind their favorite leaders and forgot they were supposed to be united behind one supreme leader—Jesus Christ. Instead of cooperating to carry out God's plan, they quarreled over who got the prominent jobs. Things were surely in a mess. So Paul wrote to them to help them get things in order (1 Corinthians 14:40).

One of the really big lessons the Corinthians needed to learn concerned spiritual gifts. The smooth operation of God's plan depended upon every church member understanding that spiritual gifts derive from God and are sovereignly distributed by the Spirit in accordance with God's plan (1 Corinthians 12:4-7). Paul taught the lesson by comparing the church to the human body. Just as each part of the body fulfills a unique and important function for the good of the whole body, even so God has gifted each member of the church so that he may perform a unique and important function for the good of the whole church (verses 12-27).

What chaos there would be in the human body, Paul suggests, if the whole body were only an eye! How would a person hear anything or smell anything? And Paul says a foot shouldn't feel slighted because it isn't a hand, for the body needs feet as well as hands. We could carry Paul's analogy further and wonder what the human body would be like if God had designed it with fifty fingers but no lips. We would have great handshakes at church, but wouldn't be able to introduce ourselves.

The application for the Corinthians was clear, and it is equally clear for us in the twentieth-century church. God's perfect plan for the church excludes gloating over prominent gifts, quarreling over the gifts, ignoring our gifts, and refusing to use our gifts in love for the good of others.

Vance Havner, evangelist and Bible teacher, tells about a thirty-year-old woman who complained to her pastor that the Lord hadn't treated her fairly.

"I'm not getting any younger, Pastor. I'm thirty years old and unmarried. Has the Lord forgotten me?" she demanded.

"Don't be so upset," the pastor advised. "You must keep in mind that God has a plan—one woman for one man and one man for one woman. That's his plan, and you can't improve on it."

"Improve on it?" the woman retorted. "I don't want to improve on it; I just want to get in on it!"

God has a plan for the church. A plan that is perfect. Critics who think they can improve on God's plan by scrapping the church and introducing something different are just kidding themselves. Rather than trying to improve on his plan, they really need to get in on it.

When our children were younger, Christmas was always an exciting time in our home. Everyone got really enthusiastic about the big event of opening presents. And we had a tradition. The presents didn't appear until Christmas morning. If we had put them out ahead of time all nicely gift-wrapped, they would have been picked up and shaken so often by our enthusiastic family members that they would have been worn out before Christmas. So each Christmas morning was loaded with excitement as we eagerly opened our presents.

I always got a special thrill from watching my daughter Becki tear away the ribbon and the wrapping and pull out her gifts. She literally exuded excitement and happiness in discovering what my wife and I had given her. But how would I have felt if her reaction had been the opposite, if she had shown no interest in opening her gifts? I would have been crushed, to say the least. And isn't our heavenly Father grieved when some of his children show no interest—or at least very little interest—in his gifts to them?

Shouldn't Christians get excited about the fact that their heavenly Father has presented them with spiritual gifts? Instead of just sitting around looking at other believers appreciate and use their gifts, these Christians need to get the ribbon off and find out what God has for them. And when they find out, they will see how practical each gift is—personally selected by the Father to be used for the work of building up the church.

Of course, even with every Christian using his spiritual gifts, the church would still have its faults. There's no denying that, for the church would still be comprised of imperfect people. But this doesn't mean we should give up on the church. We don't close down schools because a lot of students fail to get straight A's, nor do we close down hospitals because they are filled with sick people. So there's no reason to close down the church.

The church, in spite of imperfect people, is under the direct supervision of Jesus Christ, who has given life to all who are in his church. So it's bound to come out all right in the end. He's going to see to it that his church will be what he wants it to be—pure, blameless, and spotless in his sight (Ephesians 5:27).

Knowing these things gives me a lift—a confidence in the church's future. I exult in Jesus Christ, who has complete control of the church and has such a great plan for it. It is my responsibility and yours to be a part of that plan—to fit into the church's government and use the gifts he has given us for the good of the body and the winning of others to him.

Getting "things" into focus **10**

Another area which demands right thinking is prophecy, the study of God's future program. Sometimes in prophetic conferences we get the impression that the main purpose of studying prophecy is to help people fill in the empty spots in their chronological charts of the future. Or else we think it is to identify the toenail on the tenth toe of the first beast or to set a calendar date for the coming of Jesus Christ. Frankly, I don't find these purposes for prophetic study given anywhere in the Bible.

Rather, I find the Bible presenting prophecy to help us become better Christians with a value system that honors God. You see, no matter where a prophetic statement appears in the New Testament, a practical exhortation appears with it. Obviously God wants his disclosure of future events to have a dramatic effect on our values and conduct. Right thinking about the future, then, changes our attitudes and actions in the present.

When the astronauts were making their historic first trip to the moon, my wife and I were flying to Los Angeles for the Southern California Prophetic Conference to be held at the Church of the Open Door. My mind was occupied with the question of what I might use as a vitally relevant opening remark to the conference. My wife made a comment about the excitement stirred up by the moon trip, and this led to an interesting discussion about how the astronauts' travel through space compared with travel through the prophetic Scriptures. We concluded that what the trip to the moon did for the astronauts with respect to space, a trip through prophecy does for Christians with respect to time. The astronauts' perspective of the earth could never be the same again. Furthermore, it would be quite different from our perspective of the earth, for they would always remember seeing the earth, from the vantage point of the moon, as no bigger than a golf ball. Similarly, those who study Bible prophecy will gain a perspective of time which others cannot have.

Looking into the future will have a profound effect on the way you look at material *things* today. You will understand what is going to happen to material things eventually, and this will help you to set a proper value on things while struggling with a society that faces the blight of materialism.

Really, none of us is exempt from this problem of materialism. We sometimes talk about the difficulty a missionary faces in going to a primitive culture and living in a grass hut, but maybe we ought to approach the situation from a different direction. I think it may be less difficult for a missionary to live in a grass hut in a country where everyone lives in a grass hut than it is for us to live in modest homes among people who live in palatial homes. Our problem with respect to materialism is far greater than the problem confronting the person who lives in a society where the evidences of materialism are not as conspicuous.

If we got desperately honest with ourselves, we would admit there are some hymns we probably ought to take out of our hymn books, because they make hypocrites of us when we sing them. We sing, "A tent or a cottage, why should I care?/ They're building a palace for me over there." That one ought to go, for it surely doesn't fit the apparent convictions of contemporary evangelical Christianity.

Then there's the question of whether we should talk about the sacrifices we make for the sake of the gospel. What sacrifices?

Not long ago I asked a pastor of a suburban church how he applies such passages as Luke 9 where our Lord pointed out that foxes have holes and birds have nests, but the Son of man had nowhere to lay his head. The pastor replied, "I don't preach from those passages. They aren't relevant to my congregation." I can understand his problem, for you would have to search long and hard in that community to find a home under $80,000, but it seems extremely relevant.

It's easy for us to accommodate ourselves to the society in which we live. Unless we are careful, we end up with the same priorities as everyone else. We end up forfeiting eternal rewards for a taste of the so-called good life—an expensive house, a luxury car, membership in an exclusive country club, *ad infinitum.* Like Esau, who sold his birthright for a meal, we often give up the best in exchange for things that have no lasting worth. We sacrifice eternal values for the sake of temporal values because the blight of materialism in our society fouls up our priority system.

I sometimes preach from Hebrews 12:1-3 about reducing in order to run the Christian race effectively. As the text suggests, we can't run well if we carry around a lot of extra weight. So I allude to what happens to the body when it puts on a pound of fat. The fat adds a tremendous strain to the heart, the muscles, the respiratory system, and makes it difficult for a person to run. I suggest that sin-pounds have a similarly adverse effect on the spiritual life, making it difficult to run the Christian race effectively. Invariably, that message produces more converts to jogging than to spiritual exercise. Why? Because people are more concerned about being in shape physically than they are about being in shape spiritually. Apparently they don't want ill health to curtail their enjoyment of the "good life."

A similar priority system is apparent when

someone describes another person as having two or three cars, a lovely home, a camper, a boat, and everything else the heart could desire, and remarks, "The Lord has certainly blessed him." Think about that statement. If those things are the measure of the Lord's blessing upon a person, then the Mafia figures must be the most blessed people in America. Whoever gave us the idea that the possession of material things is evidence of the Lord's blessing? If things constitute his blessing, what are we to assume about devoted, dedicated Christians who possess very few things? Maybe our priority system is overdue for a biblical checkup.

So how can prophecy help us in this battle with materialism? Prophecy helps us to get "things" into focus. For example, the Apostle Peter tells us what's going to happen eventually to material things. In 2 Peter 3:10 he explains: "But the day of the Lord will come as a thief in the night; in the which the heavens shall pass away with a great noise, and the elements shall melt with fervent heat, the earth also and the works that are therein shall be burned up." In other words, *things* are going to go up in smoke someday.

Peter's prediction contains three vitally significant factors. First, the heavens—the envelope around the earth—will pass away. Can you grasp the immensity of that? In May 1974 *National Geographic* attempted to dramatize the incalculable distance. The magazine presented a series of paintings, starting with our solar system and ending with an expanse of space so great that even our Milky Way, composing 100 billion stars separated by billions of miles, was lost from view. The caption under the last painting announced: "10 billion light years." That's six trillion times ten billion miles—the distance we can see with twentieth-century telescopes. We have no idea of what lies beyond that.

What does Peter tell us about the dissolution of that limitless expanse of heavens? Very briefly, he asserts: "The heavens shall pass away with a great noise"—with a R-R-R-O-A-R-R-R! Have you ever been near a forest fire? As the flames leap up and the wind grows stronger and stronger, you have a roaring fire. That's a tiny picture of the end of the magnificent expanse of the heavens.

"And the elements shall melt with fervent heat." Peter's thoughts move from the vastness of the macrocosm to the infinitesimally small "elements" of the microcosm. The elements are the smallest things out of which all other things are formed. In Peter's day, it was supposed that the elements were earth, air, fire, and water. In the generation preceding ours, it was thought that the atom was the indivisible element out of which all things were formed. Now we realize that even the atom is divisible, so that Hebrews 11:3 becomes even more impressive to us: "Through faith [not sight] we understand that the worlds were framed by the word of God, so that things which are seen were not made of things which do appear."

Now, what does Peter predict is going to happen to the elements? He tells us they will "melt with fervent heat." Those who are involved in nuclear physics would call Peter's description an example of nuclear fission. Peter, then, portrays the destruction of the material universe from two vantage points: the vast expanse of the heavens and the infinitesimal, indivisible elements.

But Peter doesn't stop there. No, he brings it right close to home: "And the works that are therein shall be burned up." Skyscrapers costing hundreds of millions of dollars. Art treasures worth several hundred thousand each. Expensive antiques, homes, furnishings, cars, hobbies, files, collections—all will be burned up. In fact, through all of this destruction by fire, only one thing will last—*people!* Everything else will pass away, but people will last. Every person who has ever been born will live somewhere forever, either in Heaven or in Hell. This explains why God wants us to correct our priorities by putting a proper emphasis on people and deemphasizing things.

What will it take to accomplish the dissolution of the heavens, the elements, and everything man has built on the earth? Simply Jesus Christ releasing the grip he has on the world, for Colossians 1:17 suggests that in him all things are glued together.

It is my understanding that scientists can't explain what keeps the elements from blowing apart. The only explanation I can offer is Paul's revealing statement that Jesus Christ holds everything together. As the song suggests, "He's got the whole world in his hands." But one day he will let go, and it will come unglued.

Having given us a look into the future to show that someday everything above us and everything around us is going to melt and vanish in a moment, Peter urges us to think seriously about the implication of it all. In 2 Peter 3:11 he asks: "Seeing then that all these things shall be dissolved, what manner of persons ought ye to be in all holy conversation [living] and godliness, looking for and hasting unto the coming of the day of God ...?" The implication is clear—if everything we can touch, taste, smell, and accumulate is going to pass away in an instant of time, what kind of persons should we be with respect to material things?

"Lay not up for yourselves treasures upon earth, where moth and rust doth corrupt, and where thieves break through and steal: but lay up for yourselves treasures in heaven, where neither moth nor rust doth corrupt, and where thieves do not break through nor steal: for where your treasure is, there will your heart be also" (Matthew 6:19-21). These are powerful words, spoken by Jesus Christ in his Sermon on the Mount. The last clause gives the reason for the previous investment tip. Your heart will be where your treasure is. So put your treasure where you want your heart to be. If my heart's desire is the accumulation of things, there is no way that I can develop an interest in Heaven.

Spurgeon once commented to one of his church

members, upon being given a tour of the member's new palatial home, "These are the kinds of things that make dying hard." How different from Paul who desired to depart and be with the Lord (Philippians 1:23). Paul, you see, had great investments in Heaven.

But someone may object, "Matthew 6:19-21 has no bearing on my situation. I don't have to worry about piling up treasures on earth. You should have a talk with my boss. He has set my salary so low I have to bend over to pick up my paycheck. He has already made sure that I won't accumulate any treasures on earth." That objection misses the whole point of Jesus' teaching. He doesn't suggest that you have beat the problem of materialism because you don't have much. He suggests that you won't beat the problem until you stop coveting things and start putting the proper value on eternal things. After all, it's possible for a person with a very low salary to enter the home of a person with a very high salary and covet the things he sees there.

I remember when my wife and I were putting an addition on our home. I had been getting some rather grandiose ideas about what form the addition would take. Basically, I would draw up my own plans to coincide with what I had seen in somebody else's home. I wanted our add-on to be as fabulous as the "Jones'" addition. My plans called for glass partitions and a few other classy features. Then I started to build. Three times during the construction it was almost as though God stopped my hammer. I seemed to hear him caution, "Wait a minute. Why this feature? Why are you including this thing in the addition? Is it necessary? Or is it just for show?" So three times during the building of our addition, I had to change the plans.

It isn't for me to say that God works like that in regard to everyone's home. He hasn't appointed me to the position of judge. But it is for me to say we need to check up on our priorities and find out what our attitude is toward things. If we are going to lay up for ourselves treasures in Heaven, we'll have to lay aside whatever love of things we have on the earth.

> *Turn your eyes upon Jesus,*
> *Look full in His wonderful face;*
> *And the things of earth will grow strangely dim*
> *In the light of His glory and grace.*

What 11 do you think you're worth?

It used to be a humbling experience to hear that the human body was worth about forty-eight cents. Then inflation came along and the price jumped to around a dollar. Now that inflation has been with us longer than we care to think about, the human body has received a remarkable value escalation. Arthur J. Snider, science editor of the *Chicago Daily News,* reports that biochemist Harold J. Morowitz of Yale University has computed the value of elements in the human body to be $6,000,015.44. He arrived at this astounding figure after examining prices in a supply company's catalog. So it appears we are all six-million-dollar men and women, even without bionic parts.

Of course, some persons would argue that they are worth even more than six million dollars. Their excessive self-love would run the value up into the billions—maybe trillions.

As far as I am concerned, man's basic problem today isn't his failure to love himself. It seems to me that there is plenty of evidence to support Paul's prediction that in the latter days "men shall be lovers of their own selves" (2 Timothy 3:2). Perhaps it is due to the human inclination to love oneself that the Bible doesn't give us a direct command to love ourselves. Rather, we are commanded in the Word of God to love God and to love others.

On the other hand, it's possible for an individual to sell himself short—to feel worthless. A poor self-image may be the result of a complex about a physical handicap, an overweight or underweight condition, failure to achieve, inability to make friends, being too tall or too short, having a lot of pimples, or whatever. (Fortunately no person can have all of these problems at the same time.)

Again, prophecy provides the practical help we need, for it gives us the opportunity not only to get things into focus but to set a true value of ourselves as well. We can look ahead, thanks to the prophetic Scriptures, and see what God has in store for us. And in seeing this, we learn to credit everything to the grace of God. This eliminates any tendency to pat ourselves on the back, and it prohibits us from saying we aren't worth anything.

Prophecy tells me that Jesus Christ thinks so much of me, as one of his redeemed people, that he is preparing a wonderful dwelling for me in Heaven. Before he made his final preparations to die on the cross, rise from the dead, and return to Heaven, he gave me a promissory note. "I go to prepare a place for you," the note announces (John 14:2). Of course, I'm not the sole recipient of the guarantee of a heavenly home. Every Christian has the same guarantee. And what a home it will be, built personally by the Carpenter of Nazareth!

There is an interesting story in the Old Testament about what King David did for a pathetic figure of a man whose name was Mephibosheth. What a handle he was stuck with, for Mephibosheth in the Hebrew means "breathing shame." Talk about a reason for a poor self-image! Mephibosheth had more than one reason to set the price tag on himself at the discount price to beat all discount prices. Not only was his name humiliating, but when he was a child he met with a bad accident which left him "lame on his feet" (2 Samuel 9:3). Furthermore, Mephibosheth was from the wrong side of the tracks; he lived in a miserable, out-of-the-way place called Lodebar (verse 4). But that was before King David changed the picture.

Wanting to show kindness to surviving members of his friend Jonathan's family, David heard about Mephibosheth—Jonathan's son. Mephibosheth had been hiding out from David because he entertained the mistaken notion that David might want to kill him so that Mephibosheth wouldn't be around to claim the throne as King Saul's grandson.

David sent for Mephibosheth, and when Mephibosheth entered the palace he showed just how low an opinion of himself he had. He called himself "a dead dog" (verse 8). But David set a high value on Mephibosheth. He gave him land and servants, a free meal ticket to eat at the king's table as one of the king's sons, and said in effect, "Mephibosheth, you're moving in with me. My home—the palace—is your home."

What David did for Mephibosheth gives us just a little understanding of what Jesus Christ has planned for us. Someday, according to prophecy, the dwelling he is preparing for us will be ready, and he will tell us, "You're moving in with me."

That expectation alone ought to help us to set the proper value on ourselves, but prophecy puts a little frosting on the cake. It tells us that Jesus Christ himself will come someday to receive us and escort us to the dwelling he is preparing for us. Our Lord promised: "I will come again, and receive you unto myself" (John 14:3). David sent for Mephibosheth; the Son of David will come in person for us. Jesus Christ obviously has placed a high value on us.

The Apostle Paul zeroes in on Christ's coming for us in 1 Thessalonians, chapter 4. He tells us that no matter how rough things get, we can have a victorious attitude, knowing that Jesus Christ plans to unplug us from this earth someday. "The Lord himself shall descend from heaven with a shout, with the voice of the archangel, and with the trump of God," Paul explains in verse 16. Then he flashes further news bulletins across the screen: "And the dead in Christ shall rise first: Then we which are alive and remain shall be caught up together with them in the clouds, to meet the Lord in the air: and so shall we ever be with the Lord" (verses 16b, 17).

Paul's prophecy gives us a spectacular glimpse into the plans Christ has for our future. If we die before his coming, we won't miss out on the Rapture. (Some of the Thessalonians were pretty uptight about the possibility of dying before the Rapture, supposing that death would disqualify them for space travel.) At death a believer's spirit goes to be with Christ. Then, at the Rapture, his body will be raised to be united with his spirit. And the arrangement will be far better than it ever was during his life on earth. If we are alive when Christ comes in the air (1 Thessalonians 4:17) to meet us, we'll be caught up from the earth to join Jesus Christ in the air. On the way up our bodies will get an instantaneous overhaul. Every Christian will get into top physical shape quicker than you can say, "Meet me at the health spa" (1 Corinthians 15:51, 52).

I have known Christians who put a rather high value on good physical condition. They exercise every morning, follow regimented diets, work out at the gym a couple of times a week, and get a complete physical examination every six months. And I would agree that we ought to take good care of our bodies, which belong to God and are temples of the Holy Spirit. But I'm a realist. I know that eventually—if Jesus Christ doesn't return for the church before our generation passes—every Christian in our generation will die. Our bodies will be laid to rest beneath the ground. It's inevitable because our bodies have the sin sentence on them. They are deteriorating, and someday they will give out on us altogether, for "it is appointed unto men once to die" (Hebrews 9:27). So it is good to know that the Lord has planned ahead—beyond the grave. It shows that he has placed a high value on us.

At the Rapture, living Christians are going to pass from mortality to immortality, and dead Christians' bodies will pass from corruption to incorruption. That is, living bodies which are deteriorating and heading for the grave will undergo a dramatic change. That change will render it impossible for those bodies to experience any deterioration. It will make dying impossible. And dead bodies of departed Christians will undergo a resurrection, which will remove all traces of death and make it impossible for those bodies to come under the influence of death again.

Paul explained all of this to the Corinthians when he discussed the coming of Christ for the church: "The dead shall be raised incorruptible, and we shall be changed. For this corruptible must put on incorruption, and this mortal must put on immortality. So when this corruptible shall have put on incorruption, and this mortal shall have put on immortality, then shall be brought to pass the saying that is written, Death is swallowed up in victory" (1 Corinthians 15:52b-54).

There's another way to describe what is in God's plan for the Christian's body. We may say without qualification that he plans to make it conform to the kind of body Jesus Christ has—a glorified body. Paul reveals this truth in Philippians 3:20, 21: "For our conversation is in heaven; from whence also we look for the Saviour, the Lord Jesus Christ: Who shall change our vile body, that it may be fashioned like unto his glorious body, according to the working whereby he is able even to subdue all things unto himself."

Not long ago the United States Postal Service advised Americans to watch out for fraudulent offers in the mail which promise to do wonders for the human body. According to the report, Americans are being ripped off by such frauds at the annual rate of $514 million. Fat men and bald men are the most susceptible, says the Postal Service. Diet pills, hair tonics, devices to remove wrinkles and increase the length of fingernails, aphrodisiacs—all phony—are among the most appealing products offered by the con artists. Those who respond to the offers end up poorer, but just as fat, bald, and wrinkled as ever. How much better God's plan is for the Christian's body. Someday it will be perfect.

I was present at a college campfire testimonial service one balmy evening in the northern California foothills. It had been a perfectly beautiful day and the surroundings—wild flowers, stately pine trees, a nearby refreshing stream—combined to give much for which to praise the Lord. However, seated just in front of me was a blind coed. I felt sorry that she was missing the beauty that other students were giving thanks for in their testimonies. I wondered if she would have anything to say.

Sure enough, when her turn came she stood and told the group, "I haven't been able to see the beautiful things you have been giving thanks for, but on the other hand, I haven't had to look at the ugly things you have had to look at." She chuckled, then continued, "More seriously, I thank God for my blindness. You see, I have been blind from birth. I have never seen anything. My eyes are virgin eyes. And do you know what their first sight will be? Jesus Christ! I will see him when he gives me my new body eternal in the heavens, fashioned like his glorious body."

What a perspective! Why was she able to have such a great attitude in the midst of difficulties? She focused on the future.

But prophecy shows that God's plans for us include more than a new body. He is going to make us completely holy. Now we possess a sin nature, but at the Rapture we shall be like Christ—sinless. It was the elderly Apostle John who wrote: "Beloved, now are we the sons of God, and it doth not yet appear what we shall be: but we know that, when he shall appear, we shall be like him; for we shall see him as he is" (1 John 3:2).

Today God is in the process of making us Christlike. As we store the Word of God into the computer of our mind and allow it to go to work on our innermost being, we become more and more like Christ. But the process won't end until, as

John wrote, we see Jesus Christ face to face. Until then we'll carry around a sin nature.

Even the best Christians aren't perfect. Every Christian does some sinning. Only a hypocrite points to his halo and boasts about his super-spirituality. There's an interesting story about four pastors from a certain community who got away from it all for a week-long fishing trip up in the Canadian bush country. One night around the campfire they got to talking about one thing and another. Then, as the fire was getting kind of low, one of them got some sparks of his own flying. "We're a long way from home and from our church members. What do you say we let our hair down, and each of us tell what his secret sin is? I'll start it off by letting you know what mine is."

"Okay, go ahead," the others agreed.

"Well," he volunteered, "nobody in my church knows this, but occasionally I slip down to the track and place a two-dollar bet on a horse. So my secret sin is, I play the ponies."

Another pastor spoke up, "I'll take my turn now and tell you that an uncontrollable temper is my secret sin. Every once in a while I get so mad at my wife that I haul off and hit her."

The third preacher gulped and offered, "I never thought I would tell anybody this, but here goes. I keep a bottle of wine in the cellar. Every time I get into a hassle with the deacons at our board meeting, I hurry back to the parsonage, go down to the cellar, and take a nip of wine."

Silence followed the third pastor's story. The

three confessors waited to hear what the fourth pastor would relate. Finally he broke the silence. "Brethren," he announced, "I guess I have to tell you my secret sin. It is gossip. And, man, oh, man, I can't want to get home to talk to your church members."

The story is an exaggeration, of course, but it does illustrate the point that every one of us has a sin nature. But when Jesus Christ comes at the Rapture, we shall be delivered once and for all from the power and presence of sin. The prophetic Word of God guarantees that we shall be like Christ himself.

Now, doesn't all of this demonstrate clearly that God has placed a high value on every one of his children? I tell you, when I look at God's future program and see that the Lord Jesus Christ who saved me is coming for me to make me holy and to share his heavenly home with me, it puts some spiritual starch in my spine. It humbles me, too, to think that I am a worthy person to God Almighty, the God of the universe.

I had the privilege some time ago of reading William Glasser's secular book *Reality Therapy*. I appreciate getting information from people like him who come so close to some of the views the Bible teaches. Glasser suggests in his book that there are two basic human needs: 1) to love and be loved, and 2) to have self-esteem as well as esteem for others.

Can you tell me anybody in the world who is more loved than a Christian? Since a Christian is loved by God and possesses the love of God in his heart (Romans 5:5), he doesn't have to have unfulfilled needs. He can go through life feeling that God loves him—that he is a worthy person. And he can share God's love with others.

Prophecy's 12
people
perspective

Right thinking takes into consideration God's future program—what he has planned for the things around us, what he has planned for each of us, and what he has planned for others. Having considered what God's plans entail for the things around us and for us Christians, we need to think now about what lies in his plan for others.

Psalm 73 is a good starting point for our thinking about others in the light of prophecy. I got interested in this psalm when I was a seminary student. At first it puzzled me, but the more I studied it, the more I began to see others—especially the prosperous wicked—from God's perspective. As a result, Psalm 73 made a profound impact on my thinking and, I hope, on my living as well.

Written by Asaph, who was one of King David's three chief music directors and also a prophet (1 Chronicles 16:1-5; 2 Chronicles 29:30), the psalm begins on a positive note: "Truly God is good to Israel, even to such as are of a clean heart." Great! This is the kind of language we might expect from a servant of God. But Asaph really drops a bombshell in verses 2, 3 by telling us that he almost tumbled into a backslidden condition because he became envious of the prosperous wicked. They seemed to have it made—good health, smooth sailing, money coming in hand over fist. "They have more than heart could wish," Asaph concludes in verse 7.

And in spite of having it made, the prosperous wicked refused to acknowledge God's goodness. Asaph laments, "They speak loftily. They set their mouth against the heavens" (verses 8, 9).

I can almost hear Asaph's sobs when I read the first part of Psalm 73: "Lord, poor me, poor me, as I see my ungodly neighbors getting richer and richer, while I try to survive on a shoestring budget in order to be in your service. Lord, why don't you zap the prosperous wicked?"

Asaph began to wonder if there was any point in trying to live for God. So many were asking, "How doth God know? and is there knowledge in the most High?" (verse 11). It just didn't add up. Why were the righteous suffering and the unrighteous prospering? Was there any advantage to being a believer (verses 12-14)?

Is there a Christian who can't identify with Asaph in his dilemma? Probably not. We have all gone through at least one severe trial when we wondered if it pays to follow Christ. After all, the wicked seemed to be getting along just fine without God, judging from their new car, luxurious house, big raise in pay, and much more. And we have wondered like Asaph, Why doesn't God zap the prosperous wicked and vindicate us?

It must have been that question that drove Asaph to God for the answer. Verse 17 tells us he "went into the sanctuary of God; then understood...."

Where does a Christian go when he has a problem? Does he go to the medicine cabinet for a tranquilizer? Or does he go to the Lord? There is no substitute for spreading our concerns before the Lord. As someone has suggested:

> We mutter and sputter.
> We fume and we spurt.
> We mumble and grumble;
> Our feelings get hurt.
> We can't understand things.
> Our vision grows dim,
> When all that we need
> Is a moment with him.

Asaph consulted the Lord and got a perspective of the prosperous wicked that settled his questions, chased away the blues, and cured his envy. He discovered that God has a plan for the wicked—he intends to judge them in the end. A day of reckoning is coming. Asaph expresses it this way in verses 18-20: "Surely thou didst set them in slippery places: thou castedst them down into destruction. How are they brought into desolation, as in a moment! they are utterly consumed with terrors. As a dream when one awaketh ... thou shalt despise their image."

Does this mean, then, that we should rejoice in what is going to happen to the wicked? Not at all. But it certainly stabilizes our thinking to realize that God is working according to a program, which includes the judgment of the wicked. This helps us to stay calm when the wicked appear to be getting the plums while we seem to be left holding an empty bag.

The Lord Jesus Christ set an example for us in this, didn't he? Hebrews 12:2, 3 reminds us that he endured the cross, despising the shame, because of the joy that awaited him at the end. He was able to take the contradiction of sinners against himself. Why? Because of the joy that was set before him. He looked to the end and interpreted the present in light of the ultimate. He didn't interpret the present on the basis of his current circumstances.

An understanding of the future as it relates to others helps me to get under the load and help to bear the affliction of the righteous. We've heard a great deal about Americans who stand by and witness the shooting or stabbing of innocent victims. They don't want to get involved, we are told. I think we are plagued by this attitude because, as Americans, we are thinking too much about the present and not enough about the future. We are too concerned about preserving our temporal existence and not interested enough in the future that God has mapped out for us in his Word. Christians have no reason to fear taking up the cause of the afflicted—the mistreated—perhaps for righteousness' sake. We can afford to stand with them because we know the end—that God rewards the righteous and judges the wicked.

Wasn't this Moses' philosophy? Hebrews 11:24-26 reports, "By faith Moses, when he was come to years, refused to be called the son of Pharaoh's daughter; choosing rather to suffer affliction with the people of God, than to enjoy the pleasures of sin for a season; esteeming the reproach of Christ greater riches than the treasures in Egypt: for he had respect unto the recompence of the reward."

Some would consider Moses' decision ridiculous, absurd, even insane. Others wouldn't go quite that far, but they would point out that his decision didn't have the weight of common sense on its side. As Moses looked at what he had in Egypt—prestige, position, power—and looked at the poverty-stricken, beaten-into-the-ground Hebrew slaves he was thinking about identifying with, common sense would have told him to stay on the good side of the Egyptians. It would have told him to choose riches and glory and reject the will of God. It might have suggested that by staying in Egypt in the palace, he would be able to use his prestige and riches to the greater glory of God. But, as Hebrews 11 explains, Moses turned a deaf ear to common sense and chose to suffer affliction with God's people. Moses, you see, exercised farsighted faith. He looked at God's program for the future and attached the right value to God's purposes, rather than putting a value on the temporal advantages which surrounded him in Egypt.

Prophecy, then, can exert a powerful and stabilizing influence on my life in helping me to set the proper value on others, whether they are wicked or righteous.

With eternity's values in view, Lord,
With eternity's values in view,
May I do each day's work for Jesus
With eternity's values in view.

The 13
product of right thinking

"Thou wilt keep him in perfect peace, whose mind is stayed on thee: because he trusteth in thee" (Isaiah 26:3). These brief words point decisively to God's peace as the product of right thinking.

The Apostle Paul, who practiced right thinking, gives us some interesting insights into the nature of true contentment—the peace of God—in his letter to the Philippians. In 4:7 he promises, "The peace of God, which passeth all understanding, shall keep [guard] your hearts and minds through Christ Jesus." Interestingly, Paul precedes this promise with an emphasis in verses 4-6 on the process of right thinking: "Rejoice in the Lord alway: and again I say, Rejoice. Let your moderation be known unto all men. The Lord is at hand. Be careful [anxious] for nothing; but in every thing by prayer and supplication with thanksgiving let your requests be made known unto God."

The same construction occurs later in the

chapter. In verse 9 Paul promises, "The God of peace shall be with you," after emphasizing the process of right thinking in verse 8: "Finally, brethren, whatsoever things are true, whatsoever things are honest, whatsoever things are just, whatsoever things are pure, whatsoever things are lovely, whatsoever things are of good report; if there be any virtue, and if there be any praise, think on these things."

It is unmistakable, isn't it? The peace of God is the product of right thinking. And to drive home this fact with even greater forcefulness, Paul gives a personal testimony in verses 10-19 to show how the peace of God was ruling in his own life. He begins by mentioning a large gift which he had received from the Philippian church. This was not the first of such gifts he had received from the Philippian Christians, for they had given unstintingly to his needs whenever the opportunity presented itself.

Paul doesn't make a big to-do about the Philippians' gift. He says simply, "I rejoiced in the Lord greatly, that now at the last your care of me hath flourished again" (verse 10). A Christian worker can take a lesson from Paul on how to acknowledge the generous support he receives from a church. Rather than taking an undue amount of time to thank the church, rethank the members, and repeat the process *ad infinitum,* it seems advisable to do what Paul did—say thanks sincerely and briefly, and leave it there.

I was in a church on the West Coast when

the pastor advised some of the missionaries his church supported, "When you return from the mission field and speak in our church, don't spend the time we give you to minister the Word by telling us how much you appreciate our giving. Just enter the pulpit, say, 'Thanks,' and get on with the message." I think Paul, in his Philippian epistle, does what the West Coast pastor advised the missionaries to do. He is saying, "Thank you," but his main emphasis is the message he wants to communicate.

Second Corinthians 8 and 9 provides some backdrop to the kind of care the Philippians must have shown Paul. These chapters reveal that the Christians at Philippi gave liberally out of their deep poverty. I look on the Philippians' giving as one of the beautiful testimonies in the New Testament concerning the effectiveness of God's grace at work in his redeemed people. The Philippians gave so well to the relief of the hard-pressed believers in the Judean churches that Paul had to encourage them to stop giving. (When was the last time you heard a preacher tell a congregation to stop giving?) Paul states in effect, "They gave beyond their ability to give. I didn't want to take their offering because they had already given too much, but they insisted" (2 Corinthians 8:1-4). Without a doubt, the Philippians had their heads screwed on right with regard to Christian stewardship. They gave beyond their ability. They gave liberally. They must have understood the dividends of Heaven's stock market.

Having referred to their generosity, Paul continues in Philippians 4 to explain a basic, but important, principle. He explains that Christians are not dependent on what others share with them in order to be content. In verse 11 he tells the Philippians in so many words, "I am not mentioning how pleased I am with your gift so that I can squeeze some more gifts out of you. I am not bringing up this matter of giving because I can't get along on a short shoestring income, *for I have learned, in whatsoever state I am, therewith to be content.*"

In verses 12, 13 Paul assures the Philippians that he didn't engage in begging. He didn't go running around with a little tin cup, asking churches to drop some coins into it. No, indeed, for he enjoyed the peace of God. Right thinking about God and his purposes had taught Paul how to be content in any circumstances, including living under arrest in Rome.

"Content" is an interesting word, as Paul uses it. The Stoics employed it as a key word in their glossary of philosophical terms to mean "self-sufficient, needing nobody." Their attitude toward life's unpleasant circumstances was basically, Grin and bear it; keep your chin up and don't let the adversities show on you. Paul's use of "content" is, of course, quite different. He is saying to the Philippians, "I am not dependent on anybody's giving in order to get along all right. I know how to be victorious over the circumstances. It doesn't matter whether I eat well or go hungry, whether I have financial security or not. My peace comes from Christ, who gives me strength for every situation" (verses 12, 13).

Does it seem strange that Paul includes abundance in the context of being happy in spite of the circumstances? Of course, many Christians wouldn't normally consider affluence a problem, but it can be. After preaching a sermon on sacrificing for the sake of the gospel, I was approached by a wealthy lady who asked me, "Sir, have you ever thought about the problem of affluence?"

"I really can't say that I have given much thought to it," I confessed.

"Well," she continued, "it is a real problem to realize that God has given you a lot of money and the responsibility to administer it faithfully. So, sir, please have a heart for those of us who have a lot of money."

At times I have thought it must be kind of lonely to wonder if people are coming to you because of what they can get out of you because you are rich. I suppose if you were rich you would always wonder which people really cared about *you* and which people cared only about your money.

So there is the problem of affluence as well as the problem of poverty. But Paul says in verses 12 and 13, "I've known both problems, and I have caught the secret of being content. The key is in recognizing that I am not dependent on anything or anyone on earth. I have learned to be self-sufficient by drawing upon the all-sufficiency of Jesus Christ."

The principle Paul teaches in Philippians 4 needs to be learned today by a number of Christian workers who display the tin-cup attitude. Occasionally I listen to the radio and hear some Christian worker beg for money. Although he has spent a good amount of God's money to buy a half hour of radio time, he takes fifteen minutes of that time to plead with listeners to send in money so that his broadcasting of "the gospel" may continue. Quite frankly, I feel like writing to him to suggest, "Why don't you go off the air, and do God a beautiful service by not portraying him as the head of a bunch of beggars." You see, God isn't dependent on begging in order to support his work on the earth. He owns the cattle on a thousand hills. The gold and silver of the mines is all his. He doesn't ask us to beg for him; he asks us to believe him—to believe what Paul says in Philippians 4:19: "My God shall supply all your need according to his riches in glory by Christ Jesus."

Several years ago one of our faculty members from Western Conservative Baptist Seminary was participating in a Bible conference in northern Washington. At the conclusion of one of his messages, an elderly woman engaged him in conversation about a number of schools. Then she informed him that she had a significant amount of money she wanted to give to an educational cause. "Do you know of any schools that I might give to?" she asked. When our faculty member reminded her of the schools she had mentioned in their conversation, she exclaimed, "Oh no, I

wouldn't want to give my money to any of them.
All they care about is what they can get out of
me. They are just waiting for me to die, hoping to
get the rest of my money."

Then she stared at our faculty member and asked,
"Tell me, didn't I understand that you are from a
seminary?"

He replied, "That's correct."

"Western Conservative Baptist Seminary. Isn't
that the name of your seminary?" she demanded.

"That's true," he responded.

"Well, don't you people have any needs?" she
asked.

"No," answered our prof.

With a puzzled look on her face, she pressed
the matter further. "I can't believe it. With all the
educational institutions going out of business these
days I can't believe your school doesn't have any
needs."

"No, we don't have any needs," our professor
volunteered. "You see, God supplies all our *needs.*
He owns everything you have. If he wants our
seminary to have some of what you have, he will
arrange for the transfer of funds. In that way, we
would be able to say thank you to you and thank
you to him."

Upon hearing that, the woman offered, "You
know, I like you. Furthermore, I have a sister in
California who also has some money. I'm going to
write to her and tell her that I like you."

I'm kind of glad one of our faculty members was
participating in that conference instead of me. I

knew the seminary was struggling to meet salaries at that time. If I had been there, I might have pulled out a tin cup and held it close to the lady's purse. But our prof had the right philosophy, and he honored God in the way he responded to the questions.

"My God is not a beggar," Paul tells the Philippians. "If he uses you to come through on my behalf so that I eat a little better than I have in the past, I'll say thank you to God for today's menu. But if he chooses not to give me all of that, I'll tell him thanks for deciding that I should go on a diet. I've got such confidence in God's promise to meet my needs that I won't disgrace him by begging. I can be content because Jesus Christ is all-sufficient."

"Well, we don't have to give anything to Paul, since he is so content," someone in Philippi might have suggested. So Paul says in Philippians 4:14: "Notwithstanding ye have well done, that ye did communicate with my affliction." In other words, he tells the Philippians that they were doing the right thing by sharing with him in the work of the gospel.

It is not a sin to receive financial support in the ministry. It is a privilege for people to invest in the support of someone who has answered the call of God to Christian service and worthily prepared himself for that service. Paul reminds the Philippians in verse 15 that when he left Macedonia, they were the only ones who supported him. He could have unraveled a tale of woe for the rest of the chapter. He could have said, "How could the other churches in Macedonia be so callous after all I did for them? Look at what I've given up to follow Christ. You would think those other churches would show a little gratitude for what I'm sacrificing to serve Christ." Instead of complaining, though, Paul just mentions the fact that the Philippians shared with him in a financial way. And he tells them they were involved in a worthy practice.

In verse 17 Paul expresses his pleasure that the Philippians were supporting him, not because he craved their money, but because he wanted them to get some dividends from the Bank of Heaven as a result of their investment in the Lord's work.

Paul's attitude is quite different from the attitude Peter showed when he started poor-mouthing to the Lord about what it was costing to follow him. Mark 10:28 relates how Peter complained, "Lo, we have left all, and have followed thee."

I marvel at the patience of the Lord. He could have said, "Is that right, Peter? You have left all to follow me. You really have left a lot—those dirty old fish nets. Peter, they can't begin to compare with what I left. I left the ivory palaces of Heaven." But here's what he did say: "Verily I say unto you, There is no man that hath left house, or brethren, or sisters, or father, or mother, or wife, or children, or lands, for my sake, and the gospel's, but he shall receive an hundredfold now in this time, houses, and brethren, and sisters, and mothers, and children, and lands, with persecutions; and in the world to come eternal life" (verses 29, 30).

Quite a promise our Lord made to Peter. Actually, he promised him 10,000 percent interest on his investment. Even blue chip stock can't compete with that. What a phenomenal contract!

I used to read this passage in Mark and wonder, "Lord, what do you mean, 'an hundredfold ...'? I have only one house, five brothers, two sisters, and one mother." Then I read the account in the Gospels where Jesus was in a rap session with his disciples when it was reported to him that his mother and brothers were waiting for him. He pointed to the disciples and replied, "These are my mother and my brethren." In other words, he was stressing a relationship of love which binds him and his followers together in a spiritual family context.

That got through to me. I started thinking about that spiritual family relationship I have enjoyed through the years—all around the world. I understood the hundredfold factor in terms of friends who know the same Savior I serve. They are part of the spiritual family to which I belong. Mothers, brethren, sisters—and houses that are open to me all over the world. I can enter their homes, and immediately their table is my table and their home is my home. We experience a common bond of love in knowing Jesus Christ.

So Paul's desire for the believers in Philippians

4:17 encompasses dividends that defy description. I don't think for a minute that Paul would have agreed with the philosophy about giving that says to give until it hurts. That isn't a spiritual measure of giving. According to Paul's teaching in Philippians 4:17, the measure of giving is, Give until it hurts; then keep on giving until it feels good again.

I can't imagine that the little widow who dropped her last penny into the Temple treasury felt badly about giving that penny. I don't believe she moaned, "I hate to do this, but I just feel like I have to." Probably she walked up to the offering box and told the Lord, "It's the last I've got, Lord, but I know I can't outgive you. And since this is all I have, I'd better give it to you because I'm sure I am going to need some more."

Today it seems some church members drop a dollar in the offering plate and sing, "When we asunder part, it gives us inward pain." Paul's philosophy of giving runs counter to that attitude.

Finally, in his letter to the Philippians, Paul gives a testimony: "I have all" (4:18). Think of it! Paul was in a Roman prison, chained to guards, yet he announces in Philippians 4, "I have everything I need"; "I'm full"; "I'm abounding"; "I'm rejoicing"; "I'm content"; "I have all"; "This is great"; "What a mission field!" And he adds his thanks for the care package Epaphroditus delivered from the saints at Philippi (verse 18). He reports, as it were, "The box from home was terrific. The cookies and other things smelled good and tasted even better. I

am full. Everything you sent smelled good to
God, too. It was *an odor of a sweet smell, a
sacrifice acceptable, well-pleasing to God.*"

Finally, he shares verse 19 with the Philippians:
"My God shall supply all your need...." It is almost as
though he is saying, "Oh, by the way, I almost
forgot something—God is going to repay your
kindness out of his own resources. You're going
to find out, friends, that you can't outgive God."

Jim Elliot, who was martyred by Auca Indians a
number of years ago, must have cherished Paul's
words to the Philippians about God's system of
paying dividends. Jim Elliot recorded in his diary:
"He is no fool who gives what he cannot keep to
gain what he cannot lose."

There are no pockets in shrouds. We can't take
anything with us when we leave this earth to go to
Heaven, but we can send an awful lot ahead.

Right thinking involves thinking right about
the all-sufficiency of Christ to meet our needs
and direct our giving. And the product is true,
lasting contentment.